THE DEVELOPMENT OF THE INFANTRY FIGHTING VEHICLE

The Bradley Fighting Vehicle has been an integral part of the United States Army's armoured forces since the early 1980s. Its history is much longer than that, however, and is part of the broader story of armoured warfare that began with the introduction of the tank on the Western Front in 1916. From that time onward, the question for military planners has been how to integrate the infantry, the most vital part of any land-based fighting force, with armour and allow them to play a full role on the armoured battlefield.

The pioneers of this new type of warfare were most obviously the Germans, but British and French military planners had also attempted to solve the problem. In the British and French armies of the inter-war period the tendency was to subordinate armour to the infantry, producing well-armoured but slow tanks to support the infantry in their advance while also designing lighter, faster tanks that could carry out the traditional reconnaissance tasks of the cavalry. In Germany, influenced by such pioneers of armoured warfare as Heinz Guderian, a different operational approach developed. Instead of advancing at the pace of the infantry, the tanks were to spearhead the offensive in a new kind of warfare which would become known as 'Blitzkrieg'. In this doctrine small groups of infantry were equipped with *Schützenpanzerwagen* or armoured infantry vehicles capable of keeping pace with the armour and offering sufficient armoured protection to the infantry inside to allow them to fight alongside and capture objective with the tanks. Although these Panzergrenadier units (as they were known from 1942) were only even a minority of the German infantry forces in World War II, their importance and their impact upon the conduct of warfare was significant. By the end of the war a variety of fully tracked, half-tracked and wheeled vehicles had also

been introduced into the Allied a varying degrees of success in an integrate infantry forces more ful armour.

Towards of end of the war Army opted to pursue a progr development for tracked armourec to transport infantry and fulfil other battlefield roles. This was in contrast to the Soviet Union who continued to develop wheeled armoured vehicles in both the armoured personnel carrier (APC) and reconnaissance roles. In 1952 production began of the first fully tracked American APC, the M75. This could carry an infantry squad into battle in a fully enclosed armoured and tracked vehicle. The M75 saw action in the closing stages of the Korean War and was superseded in 1953 by the much cheaper M59, of which some 6,300 were produced between 1953 and 1964. The M59 also had a mortar carrier version, M84, and this proved to be a successful design. In the late 1950s the US Army began the development of an air-portable tracked armoured vehicle that would fulfil a number of battlefield roles, including APC and armoured reconnaissance.

This led, in 1959, to the production of the M113. The M113 was principally an APC, carrying eleven infantrymen into battle. It served in this role throughout the Vietnam War into the 1980s and continues to serve with the US Army in various roles to this day. The M113 was an incredibly versatile vehicle and was adapted to the armoured cavalry role, as a command vehicle, a mortar carrier, an anti-aircraft vehicle and in other specialist roles. Yet even as the M113 was entering service it was becoming clear that a new AFV was needed to survive the kind of high-intensity, Nuclear, Biological and Chemical (NBC) environment of any potential conflict with the Soviet Union. The US military recognised the need for a platform which would not only transport the infantry into battle but also allow them to engage the enemy in a fast-moving battle

(below)
The German Sd.Kfz. 251 *mittlerer Schützen panzerwagen*, first introduced in 1939, was the world's first Infantry Fighting Vehicle. It allowed the infantry to keep pace with and fight alongside the tanks in a fully protected vehicle. This version, the Sd.Kfz. 251/9, was armed with a 7.5cm gun to offer close support. (Thomas Anderson)

2172.42

(right) The M113 was the US Army's APC from 1959 into the 1980s and continues to serve alongside the Bradley in various roles to this day. Here an infantry squad disembark from their 'battle taxi' during Exercise Reforger 82. (US Army photo by Spc 4 Buck Brignano)

alongside the main battle tanks. Alongside the development of the MBT-70 between the Americans and Germans, there was also a programme to develop a Mechanized Infantry Combat Vehicle (MICV-70). Whereas the former led, in a convoluted way, to the Leopard 2 and M1 Abrams, the MICV project was, as we shall see, abandoned in 1968 as the vehicle could not be airlifted.

In 1967 the infantry/armour doctrines that dominated NATO armies were dealt a shocking blow when the Soviet BMP (*Boevaya Mashina Pekhoty* or Infantry Fighting Vehicle IFV) was revealed in public for the first time. In common with the Americans, Soviet planners assumed that any future battlefield would be dominated by NBC weapons and the combined properties of a light tank and an armoured personnel

carrier would best allow the infantry to continue to fight effectively alongside main battle tanks. Previously Soviet APCs, like their American counterparts, were designed to transport their infantry to the battle area, disembark them and then retreat to a safe distance. The requirement for the BMP, drawn up in the late 1950s, called for a radical change of tactics. The infantry would be able to fight from within their vehicle and a fast-paced assault, alongside tanks, would carry all before it. The vehicle needed to offer protection against .50cal heavy machine gun rounds and also allow every member of the incumbent infantry squad to fire their weapons from within squad compartment. The vehicle would also be armed with a 73mm cannon to engage infantry emplacements and the like, as well as an Anti-Tank Guided Missile (ATGM)

(below) The FV432 was the British Army's equivalent of the M113 and served in the APC role from 1962. (MP Robinson)

with which to engage enemy armour. The original prototype of the BMP was built in 1964 and it was first issued for testing to the Red Army for the following year. The first model went into serial production in 1966 and began equipping units of the Red Army the following year. At the same time large numbers of wheeled BTR-60 APCs were introduced, signalling the Soviet's determination to field an entirely mechanised army.

(left) The BMP marked a major turning point in armoured warfare when it was introduced in the mid 1960s. Here a prototype with the Tamanskaya Motor Rifle Division exercises in the snow during the winter of 1965/66. (James Kinnear)

(centre) A column of Soviet BMP-1 travels through the mountains of Soviet Central Asia. Soviet propaganda of the 1970s and 80s stressed the sheer number of BMPs and other armoured vehicles available to the armies of the Warsaw Pact. (TASS)

(below) The two principal weapons systems of the US Armoured Divisons in the 1970s: the M60 Main Battle Tank and the M113 APC. These two were photographed during the Reforger 79 exercises in Germany. (NARA)

(right) One of the XM-723 prototypes is offloaded from a YC-15 aircraft at Yuma Air Base, AZ, in December 1975. (US Army photo by Charles P. Connally)

THE DEVELOPMENT OF THE BRADLEY

By the early 1960s the development and deployment of tactical nuclear missiles by both the United States and the Soviet Union had forced military planners on both sides of the Iron Curtain to look again at infantry tactics. In 1964 the US Army invited bids for the development of the new MICV-65 (Mechanized Infantry Combat Vehicle-65). The Pacific Car and Foundry's XM701, which used many parts in common with the M109 Self-Propelled Howitzer, won the competition, but by 1968 the design had been abandoned amidst concerns that it would not be able to keep pace with the proposed MBT-70 and was too heavy to be airlifted in a C-141 transport aircraft. Around the same time the new West German Marder I was also evaluated, but it was considered too heavy and too costly for American service.

The demands of the war in Vietnam put many US defence plans on hold, but the war also underscored the need to look again at the 'battle taxi' concept. In Vietnam the threat of mines and RPGs had led to many infantrymen choosing to ride atop, rather than inside, their M113s, while the need for the infantry to assault the objective in their APCs had led to the development of the M113 ACAV (Armored Cavalry). As we have seen, the unveiling of the new Soviet BMP underscored the unsuitability of the M113 for any future conflict in Europe. In 1967 the Ford Motor Company (FMC), the manufacturer of the M113, had offered the Army the XM765 AIFV (Armored Infantry Fighting Vehicle), which was essentially a redesigned M113. It was visually similar to the M113 but had a single-man turret equipped with either the 25mm Oerlikon or 20mm Rheinmetall cannon. The vehicle was rejected as it was insufficiently armoured and could not keep pace with the planned new M1 Main Battle Tank, although it would later form the basis of the Dutch YPR-765.

The Army had maintained its interest in the MICV project throughout the 1960s. In 1965 a second project, entitled 'Mechanized Infantry Combat Vehicle Family' was initiated to run in parallel with the MBT-70 project. This was abandoned in 1972 with the collapse of the MBT project and that year proposals were invited to develop a new vehicle. Pacific Car and Foundry, Chrysler Corporation and FMC all threw their hats into the ring and late that year FMC won the contract to develop a prototype IFV, the XM723 MICV. The XM723 had design features which originated with the US Marine Corps' LVTP-7 and was thus significantly larger than the M113. It was powered by the Cummins VTA903 diesel engine and could swim using its 21-inch wide single-pin tracks. The vehicle had aluminium armour proof against projectiles up to 14.5mm in calibre, while spaced laminate steel armour was added to the sides and rear of the vehicle. It was crewed by three – a commander, gunner and driver – and could carry a fully equipped eight-man infantry squad. Six firing ports and periscopes, located at the sides and rear of the vehicle, were designed to allow the infantry squad to observe the battlefield and fire their weapons from within the vehicle. It was originally armed with a turret-mounted 20mm cannon (both the M139 and XM236 were installed on the prototypes) as the specified 25mm Bushmaster cannon was not yet available, and it was also equipped with a coaxial 7.62mm machine gun. Importantly, at this stage the vehicle did not yet have any specific anti-armour capability. The XM723 was much more heavily armoured and had greater performance than the M113, weighing 43 tons and with a top road speed of some 45mph, but it was also much more expensive.

Testing of the XM723 prototypes was successful and in 1976 the Army established the Larkin Task Force to determine its future requirements for the MICV programme. As well an infantry fighting vehicle, the Army now also required a new cavalry scout and reconnaissance vehicle to replace the M551 Sheridan. The XM800 Armored Reconnaissance Scout Vehicle had been cancelled and the XM723 vehicle was to be the basis for a new AFV that could fulfil both roles. The principal change to the XM723 was a new two-man turret armed with a 25mm Bushmaster cannon and TOW missiles providing the all-important anti-armour capability. The new configuration for the infantry vehicle also included three Light Anti-Tank Weapons (LAW) stowed in the squad compartment The scout vehicle was essentially the same as the MICV but for the removal of the firing ports along the hull sides and additional storage space for ten instead of five TOW missiles.

In May 1977 the XM723 was re-named the XM2, with the cavalry reconnaissance version named the XM3. The basic chassis, known as the Fighting Vehicle System (FVS) Carrier, was also to be the basis of the proposed Multiple Launch Rocket System (MLRS). FMC delivered the first prototypes of the XM2 in December 1978 with a further six delivered in the spring of the following year. The development of the XM2/3 was not straightforward and faced political as well as military questioning over cost, size and the vehicles' ability to survive on the NBC battlefield. In 1978 plans to develop the M113 as an IFV were finally dropped and in the following year the XM2/3 passed the Army Systems Requisition Review Council and were designated the M2 Infantry Fighting Vehicle and M3 Cavalry Fighting Vehicle. On 1 February 1980 procurement for service production was approved by the Secretary of Defense and in October 1981 the vehicle was formally adopted and named as the M2/M3 Bradley Fighting Vehicle, after General Omar Bradley, the

hero of the Normandy campaign, who had died earlier that year. Originally the M3 was to have been named after General Jacob L. Devers, but as the two vehicles were so similar it was decided that a common name across the Bradley Fighting Vehicle (BFV) family would be more appropriate. In 1982 the first Bradleys were delivered to the 41st Infantry Regiment, based at Fort Hood, TX, and in the following year they began to equip the 3rd Infantry Division (Mechanized) in Germany.

The XM723 and BFV projects were controversial for several reasons. First, doubts were raised over the operational assumptions made about the MICV vehicle itself. The BFV was clearly not well protected enough to face enemy armour, but it afforded the infantry a degree of protection and, more importantly, an offensive capability that the M113 or similar APCs simply couldn't provide. In the 1970s doubts were also raised over the cost, but from 1981, with the increased military spending of the Reagan administration, these voices became less influential. More importantly perhaps critics questioned the wisdom and safety of the entire IFV concept: was it sensible, for example, to combine combat and transport functions, forcing soldiers to share space with volatile ammunition? The Bradley's aluminium armour was described as a death-trap, with the dangers of the toxic vapours released when the vehicle was hit not exposed by the test dummies the Army had apparently crewed the vehicle with during trials. In 1984 the House Armed Services Committee told the then Secretary of Defense Casper Weinberger that they were 'dismayed' and 'deeply disturbed' by the Army's apparently cavalier attitude to soldiers' safety. Nevertheless, the Army defended the BSV vehemently and looked to procure some 7,000 Bradley at a cost of more than $13 billion over the next decade.

(below) An early M3 Bradley CFV of 2-6 Cavalry is tested at Fort Knox, KY, in January 1983. Note the colourful temperate MERDC camouflage scheme. (US Army photo by Steve Catlin)

(above) An M2 fires down range at Fort Benning, GA, in June 1983. Note the two firing ports for M231s in the middle of the hull operated by members of the seven-man infantry squad. (US Army photo by Spc 5 Bobby Mathis)

BRADLEY DESCRIBED: M2/M3

The vehicle that was delivered to the US Army in 1983 represented a major stepchange in the United States' warfighting capability. The Bradley was significantly heavier, larger, faster, better-protected, and more deadly than the M113. Bradley production was swift, signalling the Reagan Administration's determination to re-arm America against the Soviet Union. A hundred Bradleys (75 M2 IFV and 25 M3 CFV) were produced in 1980-81, rising to four hundred the next year and then six hundred each over the next two years. In 1984-85 a further 680 were produced.

From the outside the M2 and M3 were virtually identical. The difference lay in the elimination of the hull firing ports and hull roof periscopes on the latter. In every other respect the exteriors of the two vehicles were identical. Internally too they were largely the same. In both the driver sat at the front, offset to the left. The large driver's hatch could be locked in the open position, affording him protection from overhead shell bursts while driving with the hatch open. The driver's middle periscope could be fitted with the passive AN/VV2 night lens for night driving. The driver was connected to the squad compartment by a passageway in which, in the M2, two members of the seven-man infantry squad sat. They had two hull firing ports fitted with the M231, a compact version of the M16A1 rifle modified to only fire on automatic. The two-man turret, identical on both vehicles, was offset to the right. The M242 Bushmaster cannon could fire Armour-Piercing Discarding Sabot – Tracer (APDS-T) and High Explosive – Incendiary and training (HEI-T) rounds. There was also a M240 7.62mm machine gun mounted coaxially. The Bushmaster cannon was fully stabilised, allowing the Bradley to fire on the move. The gunner aimed the Bushmaster cannon through his Gunner's Integrated Sight Unit (ISU) which had a thermal imaging night sight, which could also see through fog, smoke and the like. This system alone gave the Bradley an important edge over its erstwhile

(right) 1-41 Infantry (Mechanized), 2nd Armored Division, based at Fort Hood, TX, was the first unit to be equipped with the M2 in 1982. (NARA)

opponents and accounted for one tenth of the production costs of each vehicle. The turret was also equipped with a dual BGM-71 TOW missile launcher and two banks of four smoke grenade dischargers on the front of the turret. The turret housed the vehicle commander and the gunner.

The rear of the squad compartment on the M2 had space for five infantrymen, although usually only four seats were fitted and the space used for additional stowage. These men too had access to firing ports equipped with the M231 automatic rifle. The rear of the M2 also housed an additional two man-portable TOW launchers, five additional TOW rockets, five M72A2 LAW launchers and 600 rounds of 25mm ammunition. The principle difference between the M2

and M3 was the configuration of this rear compartment. In the M3 there were only two rear-facing seats for the scouts and the remainder of the space was utilised for the stowage of an additional ten TOW missiles and 1,200 25mm rounds. On the early M3s the hull firing ports were simply blanked off by a riveted circular metal plate and the periscopes on the right-hand side of the hull covered over as that side of the M3 was given over to the additional missile stowage. On both the M2 and the M3 the infantry squad or scouts could exit the vehicle by the large rectangular hatch at the rear. Within that hatch was an oval-shaped door. On both the M2 and the M3 there were two additional firing ports in the rear hatch.

(left) An M2 or M3 during Exercise Shadow Hawk 87 held in Jordan in September that 1987. From this angle, and with no unit identification given, it is impossible to determine whether this is an IFV or CFV. (US Army photo by Pfc. Prince Hearns)

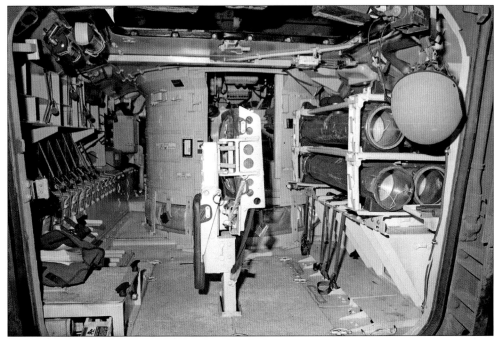

(left) The interior of the M3 CFV of 3-1 Cavalry. Note the additional TOW missiles on the right-hand side and the rearward facing scout seat, which has been folded down. On the left-hand side are the empty racks for the 25mm ammunition boxes. (US Army photo by Spc. Diana Lindsey)

M2A1/M3A1

Like all modern armoured fighting vehicles the baseline Bradley Fighting Vehicle was designed to incorporate a series of improvements and upgrades as it progressed through its service life. As soon as the Bradley was in full production work began on the so-called Block I Improvements. These improvements were a result of field reports from the first units equipped with the Bradley and research by the FCM and the Army Tank Automotive Command (TACOM). The changes consisted of three main design features: an improved TOW launcher, the installation of a Gas Particulate Filter Unit (GPFU) for enhanced NBC protection, and a raft of smaller designed changes introduced as a result of experiences in the field with the first-production Bradleys.

By the early 1980s the introduction of the Warsaw Pact's New third-generation MBTs, the T-64 and T-72, rendered the original TOW missile obsolete. In late 1984 the new BGM-71D TOW-2 missile was fitted to new prototypes, designated M2E1 and M3E1, at the Aberdeen Proving Ground. The idea of replacing the twin-tube launcher with two separate launchers was considered but quickly rejected The installation of the GPFU was also introduced on the M2E1 and M3E1. In the original Bradley NBC protection was provided solely by the crew's own personal NBC suits and gas masks. The GPFU allowed the driver, gunner and commander on the M2E1 and all five members of the scout squad in the M3E1 to connect their gas masks to a central filter unit. The remaining members of the infantry squad in the M2E1 retained their own filters in their personal NBC protection as the US Army planners, unlike their counterparts in the Soviet Union, considered that the need to frequently open the rear hatch and for the squad to dismount would render a filtration system for the entire vehicle unnecessary.

As well as these major changes, there were a raft of minor design improvements made to both the inside and the outside

(right) A clear view of a CFV, upgraded to M3A1 standard, of 3rd Armored Cavalry Regiment during Operation Desert Shield in April 1992. The blanked off hull firing ports of the M3 are clearly visible, but note this vehicle lacks the driver's hatch periscopes guard and still has the older style rear turret stowage. (US Army photo by SSgt. Ruark)

(right) Another refurbished M3A1, this time of HQ Troop, 3-1 Cavalry, is welcomed by Major General Thomas Carney, commander of 5th Infantry Division, to Fort Polk, LA, in April 1990. This vehicle clearly has the new TOW-2 launcher and a fresh coat of the new three-colour NATO camouflage scheme, but lacks the driver's hatch periscopes guard and still has the turret grenade boxes. (US Army photo by Spc Diana Lindsey)

(left) A brand new M2A1 of 2-7 Infantry, 24th Infantry Division (Mechanized) at the National Training, Fort Irwin, CA, in November 1988. This IFV features the driver's hatch periscopes guard, while the turret grenade boxes have been replaced by stowage straps. (NARA)

of the Bradley as part of the Block I Improvements. On the new CFV four periscopes installed on the upper hull cargo hatch replaced the three periscopes in the roof of the M3. The two periscopes on the right side of the hull, where the additional TOW missiles were stowed, were also dclcted, while the two scout seats were also relocated directly under the cargo hatch. In the IFV the seating arrangements for the infantry squad in the rear of the vehicle were changed. A seventh seat for an additional squad member was added behind the turret. There were also several survivability changes introduced. Spall blankets were added around the turret cage to protect the rounds stored their for the main gun, while the upright fuel cell in the rear of the vehicle was replaced by an additional fuel cell in the floor. Additional ammunition stowage was provided under the side armour, while mines, flares and grenades were moved to reinforced bustle boxes at the rear of the vehicle, allowing for the removal of the grenade box from the turret front. The rear turret stowage bin was also redesigned to have a straight back as opposed to the sloping one on the M2 and M3. The M2E1 and M3E1 also had additional smoke launchers fitted on the turret, but these do not appear to have been fitted to production vehicles. A step guard was also introduced over the driver's hatch periscopes.

The Block I Improvements were introduced sequentially, with the GPFU being first and incorporated into new vehicles leaving the production line from May 1986. The new TOW-2 missiles were fitted from early 1987. The Bradleys with the Block I Improvements were known as M2A1 and M3A1 respectively. The most important modifications – the new TOW launcher and the GFPU – were retrofitted to earlier vehicles, but many of the smaller design improvements appear not to have been fitted. This makes identification of new-production M2A1/M3A1s in the field quite difficult. Photographs show that many of the original design features, such as the turret grenade stowage and the older sloping rear turret stowage bustle, remained on vehicles upgraded to A1 standard, even up to their deployment in 1990/91 to the Persian Gulf.

(left) A great photo illustrating the problems of differentiating the M2/M3 from the M2A1/M3A1. Although the driver's hatch periscopes guard, squad compartment roof, TOW launcher front cover and all the other minor differences between the two are obscured, the date of the photograph, April 1990, and the three-tone NATO camouflage identify this as an A1 standard vehicle. In fact, this is another of the refurbished M3A1s delivered to 5th Infantry Division. (US Army photo by Spc Diana Lindsey)

M2A2/M3A2

As we have seen, by the mid 1980s the Bradley Fighting Vehicle was coming in for a fair degree of criticism both in the press and in Congress. As early as 1984 the US Army began a programme to develop a High Survivability version of the Bradley which would address concerns about its armour protection and the dangers posed to the crew by the storage of ammunition inside the vehicle. The Army tested two versions using prototypes of the M2 and M3: a High Survivability Version (HSV), which was fitted with reactive armour, additional steel plate on the hull and turret, a spall liner throughout the interior of crew compartment and new stowage arrangements for the 25mm ammunition and the TOW missiles; and an Advanced Survivability Version (ASV), which also had its fuel tanks and stowed TOW missiles moved to the exterior of the vehicle, while the internal stowage of the 25mm ammunition was compartmentalised. Both versions saw a weight increase of some seven tons over the Bradley baseline vehicle. Both these versions were then subjected to a number of live-fire and operational tests. The results of the tests, presented to a subcommittee of the House Committee on Armed Forces on 17 December 1987, led to several recommendations for improving the Bradley.

First, the tests had showed that even the appliqué armour fitted to the HSV and ASV were not sufficient to protect the Bradley against the 30mm high-velocity cannon fitted to the new Soviet BMP-2 and even heavier armour was recommended to the committee. The Army also recommended the adoption of Explosive Reactive Armour (ERA) on the Bradley, the fitting of spall liners throughout the crew compartment, and a re-stowage of the ammunition. The modifications would increase the Bradley's weight by some 30 per cent and increase the programme's total cost by some $1.6 billion. These recommendations led, in May 1988, to the M2A2 and M3A2. In 1990 Congress approved the upgrade of all

M2A1 and M3A1 to A2 standard. Between 1988 and 1994 3,053 M2A2 and M3A2 were produced from new, while most of the existing 3,671 AO and A1 standard vehicles were also upgraded.

The A2 modifications brought in a number of important and visible changes to the Bradley. Most obvious were the two laminated quarter inch-thick steel appliqué armour plates with an inch gap between them along the hull sides. These necessitated the removal of the port firing stations on the M2, with only those in the rear hull hatch remaining. Additional armour was also added to the hull front to protect the transmission. On production M2A2/M3A2 the ERA tiles were not fitted and indeed the tiles did not become available until October 1993 when a contract was awarded to Lockheed Martin and the Israeli Rafael Development Agency. The trim vane on the front of the hull, which had led to several accidents while swimming, was removed and replaced with a different design and additional armour plating was added to the engine access hatch and the hull front. The removal of the trim vane also allowed for the repositioning of the headlights, which received a new armoured housing. The appearance of the turret was also transformed with new appliqué armour, while the smoke grenade boxes were relocated to the underside of the turret front and the armoured shroud removed from the coaxial M240 machine gun. Inside the Bradley the crew sighting arrangements changed again. In the original HSV five infantry sat in the rear of the IFV, while a sixth squad member sat to the rear of the corridor leading from the driver's position to the squad compartment. As a result of the live-fire tests, on production M2A2s the number of infantrymen was again raised to seven, with three seated on bench seats either side of the squad compartment and a seventh at the front of the side corridor, immediately behind and with his back to the driver. The earlier Dragon anti-tank missile which could be carried in the IFV instead of additional TOW missiles was

(right) A side view of an M2A2 showing the new armour configuration. This is a vehicle of 1st Brigade, 24th Infantry Division (Mechanised). The division re-equipped with M2A2s after Operation Desert Storm, but retained the CARC Tan camouflage as part of the US Army's Rapid Deployment Joint Task Force. (US Army photo by Don Teft)

(left) An infantry squad debus from an M2A2 during training at Fort Hood, TX, in 1999. The thickness of the side appliqué armour is evident from this angle. (US Army photo by John Byerly)

replaced by the Javelin ATGM at this time, enabling either five TOWs or three TOWs and two Javelin launchers to be carried. In the CFV HSV the two scouts sat at the rear of the vehicle with their backs facing the rear ramp, but in the production M3A3 they sat on a bench seat at the rear left-hand side of the vehicle.

Combat loaded, the weight of the BFV had increased from some 25 tons to 30 tons with the A2 standard modifications. The Army tests had also identified problems with the Bradley's transmission, which were only made worse by this increase in weight. Therefore, from May 1989, the 500hp Cummins diesel engine was replaced by the 600hp hp VTA-903T turbo-charged diesel engine.

It is interesting to note the changes to the Bradley that were considered in 1985-1987 but not adopted in the A2 configuration.

The integrated sight unit which, as we have seen, was the single most costly piece of equipment fitted on the Bradley was not upgraded, despite repeated concerns over its reliability. Moreover, the Bradley remained unequipped with a comprehensive NBC survival system. While the GPF introduced with the A1 upgrades had provided an integrated system for the driver, gunner and commander on the IFV and the entire crew on the CFV, concerns remained among Bradley units and senior US Army generals that the Bradley would be unable to conduct sustained operations on a contaminated battlefield. Although the 1987 report concluded that 'if these vehicles encounter chemical agents on the battlefield, the Bradley may be unable to fight with and support the Abrams tank', no effort was made to address this issue as part of the A2 modifications.

(below) Many M2A2 and M3A2 were still in service at the start of Operation Iraqi Freedom. Here an M3A2 ODS of Charlie Troop, 1-4 Cavalry, 1st Infantry Division pauses near Ad Dwr, Iraq, in November 2004. The CFVs have the side armour ERA tiles of the BUSK (Bradley Urban Survival Kit) I fitted. (USAF photo by SSgt. Shane A. Cuomo)

(right) A good view of a M2A2 ODS from 3-15 Infantry, 3rd Infantry Division (Mechanized) at Fort Stewart, GA, in 1997. You can clearly see the laminate appliqué. The Bradley is also fitted with the MILES training equipment. (US Army photo by Don Teft)

M2A2 ODS/M3A2 ODS

Operation Desert Storm in 1991 proved to be a vindication for the much-maligned Bradley Fighting Vehicle. As we shall see, during the 100 hours of ground combat, the Bradley destroyed more Iraqi AFVs than the Abrams MBT and only three vehicles were lost to enemy action. Nevertheless, Operation Desert Shield did reveal a number of shortcomings in the Bradley's design and performance. Some units complained it was simply too large and began experimenting with the recently introduced High Mobility Multi-Purpose Wheeled Vehicle (HMMWV) as a scout vehicle. The main gunsight, long recognised as a problem with the Bradley, was the other element of the vehicle that was clearly in need of an overhaul.

As a result of analysis following the end of the First Gulf War a number of improvements were introduced to the A2 standard vehicle. These included a new eye-safe carbon dioxide laser rangefinder,

(below) Scouts from 1-4 Cavalry, 1st Infantry Division, prepare to mount their M3A2 ODS at Forward Operating Base Mackenzie near Samarra, Iraq, in October 2004. These Bradleys are fitted with the Bradley Reactive Armor Tiles (BRAT) on both the side appliqué armour and the turret. (USAF photo by SSgt. Shane A. Cuomo)

a new tactical navigation system (TACNAV) incorporating a global positioning system (GPS) and digital compass, Combat Identification Panels (CIP) mounted on the rear and hull sides, a driver's thermal viewer, and a countermeasure device. There were a few external changes, the most notable being a new style opening mechanism for the driver's hatch. There were other internal changes, including a heater for the Meals Ready to Eat (MRE) ration packs. The proposed missile countermeasure device does not appear to have been fitted, however, to production A2 ODS vehicles. 1,432 Bradleys were brought up to this standard from 1994 and they are referred to as the M2A2 ODS and M3A2 ODS. The combat weight of the vehicle increased to 35.4 tons as a result of these improvements. From around 2000 further changes were introduced to integrate the A2 ODS vehicles more fully into the digital battlefield. The Force XXI Battle Command

Brigade and Below (FBCB2) programme was applied across all the major components of the US Army's armoured force, including the Abrams MBT and the AH-64 Apache attack helicopter. This system includes a Blue Force Tracker, allowing commanders to instantly know the deposition of friendly forces, through an Enhanced Position Locating Reporting System. This version of the Bradley is known as the M2A2 ODS SA/M3A2 ODS SA (Situational Awareness).

The M2A2 ODS/M3A2 ODS version of the Bradley is marketed by BAE Systems as 'well positioned for foreign military sales', but export of the Bradley has thus far been limited to Saudi Arabia and the Lebanon.

Some 400 M2A2 ODS had been delivered to the Saudis by 2015. Saudi interest in the Bradley dated back to 1983 when the vehicle was first demonstrated to them, and the first order was placed six years later. The Bradleys of the Royal Saudi Arabian Army have recently been engaged in Yemen against Houthi rebels and some forty are reported to have been lost to enemy action. In August 2017 the US delivered the first of 32 Bradleys to the Lebanon which was part of a comprehensive military package of over $100 million dollars including M198 howitzers, HMMWVs and Cessna aircraft armed with Hellfire missiles.

(above) An M2A2 ODS of 1-26 Infantry, 2nd Brigade Combat Team, 1st Infantry Division prepares for deployment to Iraq at the Hohenfels Training Area in Germany in March 2006. (US Army photo by Spc. Bill Brothers)

(left) An M2A2 ODS of 1-26 Infantry, 2nd Brigade Combat Team, 1st Infantry Division, during Exercise Noble Shephard, conducted at Hohenfels prior to the unit's deployment to Iraq. (US Army photo by SSgt. Ricky R. Melton)

(right) New M3A3s of
2-5 Cavalry, 1st Cavalry
Division, during
Operation Iron Fury,
designed to pacify
the Baghdad suburb
of Sadr City in August
2004. The Bradley are
equipped with a full
set of Bradley Reactive
Armor Tiles (BRAT). (US
Army photo by Cpl.
John Wright)

M2A3/M3A3

In 1994 United Defense Limited Partnership (which would become in time part of BAE Systems) was awarded a contract to develop a fully digitised Bradley that could operate effectively alongside the latest M1A2 Abrams MBT. This was part of the US Army's vision for a new structure known as 'Force XXI' which had originated in March that year. The new Bradley would also incorporate improvements highlighted from experience gained in the First Gulf War. The first prototype M2A3s and M3A3s were delivered to the Army in November 1998 and entered service in April 2001. Just over a year later the vehicle was approved for full-rate production. In February 2005 an order was made for another 120 A2 ODS standard vehicles to be upgraded, followed four months later by a further order for 450. By October 2010 3,390 Bradleys had been upgraded to A3 standard.

(below) An M2A3
of 3-69 Armor, 1st
Armored Brigade
Combat Team, 3rd
Infantry Division,
crosses a river during
Exercise Heidersturm
Shock near Storkau,
Germany, in June 2015.
Note the stowed CIV
at the rear, right-hand
side of the turret. (US
Army photo by Markus
Rauchenberger)

The principal change to the Bradley A3 version was the incorporation of a system intended to provide increased situational awareness and digital command and control capabilities necessary to provide information superiority to the 'dominant maneuver force' of the Bradley and the Abrams. These systems were developed and tested from 1997 as part of the 'Advanced Warfighting Experiments' conducted at the National Training Centre at Fort Irwin, CA and led to the adoption of the Force XXI Battle Command Brigade and Below (FBCB2) communications platform. The Basis of Issue document for the BFV A3 called for a 'core electronic architecture' comprising a 1553 Databus Central Processor to control a sophisticated system of digital fire control, communications and navigation software. The principal external change was the addition of a Commander's Independent

Viewer (CIV) on the right-hand side of the turret behind the commander's cupola. Linked to the Improved Bradley Acquisition System (IBAS), it provides a forward-looking infrared and an electro-optical/TV imaging system. The IBAS includes both direct-view optics and the eye-safe laser rangefinder. It enables the commander to scan for and detect targets independently of the gunner while under armour. All of this is backed up by fire control software which takes in the environmental factors and ammunition type to automatically elevate the gun for range. The software can track two targets simultaneously, enabling the TOW-2 launchers to engage and destroy moving targets. All this information is available to the commander via a new Commander's Tactical Display (CTD). As well as improving the Bradley's lethality, the A3 programme also improved its protection by adding titanium turret and hull roof protection against overhead airburst artillery fragmentation. Mobility too was enhanced by improvements to the driver's thermal viewer and the periscopes in the driver's hatch, as well as a new Position Navigation System (PNS).

The M2A3 and M3A3 have undergone a number of further improvements during their twenty years of front line service. During the Iraq War the Bradley Urban Survivability Kit (BUSK) was introduced to protect the vehicle in urban environments. This consisted of a set of improved ERA tiles, as well as spotlight, mesh guards for the vehicle's optics, non-conductive brush guards designed to clear fallen electrical lines, and underbelly armour to protect against Improvised Explosive Devices (IEDs). Transparent shields, like those fitted to the Abrams, were also fitted around the commander's and gunner's cupola as part of the BUSK II package. By October 2008 more than 600 Bradleys had received the BUSK II upgrade. In 2012 the first BUSK III kits, incorporating a blast-proof fuel cell, blast-resistant driver's seat, turret survivability system and an emergency ramp release, were fitted to 236 Bradleys stationed in Korea. In March 2013 BAE Systems receive an additional contract worth $16.6 million to convert M3A3 to M2A3, also adding an additional seat in the squad compartment for a seventh infantryman.

The increase in weight as a result of the BUSK package was considerable, some three tons, and in 2014 a major upgrade was planned to incorporate these changes in the Bradley fleet as part of the Engineering Change Proposal (ECP) I and II packages. These were to include new tracks and suspension, a new power pack and transmission improvements delivering 800hp, an Automatic Fire Extinguishing System, anti-IED electronic countermeasures, a reinforced driver's seat, and improved Situational Awareness, including an improved FBCB2 and Blue Force Tracker. The first contract for the ECP I, concerning the suspension and tracks primarily, for $49.1 million was awarded in July 2017 with a completion date for 276 BFVs by April 2019.

Vehicles that receive both ECP upgrades will be known as BFV A4. In June 2018 BAE Systems was awarded a further contract worth $347 million to supply 473 M2A4 and M7A4 Bradley Fire Support Team Vehicles (BFIST). This was followed in October 2019 with a $269 million contract for another 168 M2A4s. Further improvements planned include a new generation of TOW missiles, the BGM-71F TOW 2B.

(below) A Bradley Engineer Squad Vehicle (BESV) of 91st Engineer Battalion, 1st Armored Brigade Combat Team, 1st Cavalry Division, during Exercise Combined Resolve in December 2018. This vehicle is based on the M3A2 and can be fitted with various engineering components, such as mine rollers. Note the Commander's Protection System around his cupola and the new-style tracks, part of the ECP I upgrades. (US Army photo by Staff Sgt. Ron Lee)

1. M3, 2nd Squadron, 6th Cavalry Regiment, Fort Knox, KY, January 1983.
This early M3 wears a Summer Verdant MERDC (Mobility Equipment Research and Development Center) camouflage of Forest Green FS34079, Light Green FS34151, Sand FS30277 and Black FS37038. The unit was the first to receive the M3 CFV and was involved in testing this a nd the M1 Abrams at the United States Army Armor School at Fort Knox.

((US Army photo by Steve Catlin)

COLOUR PROFILES BY SLAWOMIR ZAJACZKOWSKI

2. M2, 1st Battalion, 7th Infantry Regiment, Exercise Central Guardian, Germany, January 1985. This M2 was finished in overall Forest Green FS34079. Exercise Central Guardian was the first of the annual REFORGER exercises in which the Bradley was deployed in battalion strength. 1-7 Infantry operated alongside the M1 Abrams of 3-69 Armor as part of the 3rd Brigade, 3rd Infantry Division, testing the new vehicles in cold weather conditions.

3. M2A1, unknown unit, Exercise Centurion Shield, Germany, January 1990.
This M2A1, identifiable by the new larger rear stowage rack, has a temporary whitewash applied over its Forest Green FS34079 camouflage. The whitewash camouflage applied to US AFVs, notably during the Field Training Exercise (FTX) components of the REFORGER exercises in 1985 and 1990, was soon washed and worn away in the field.

3

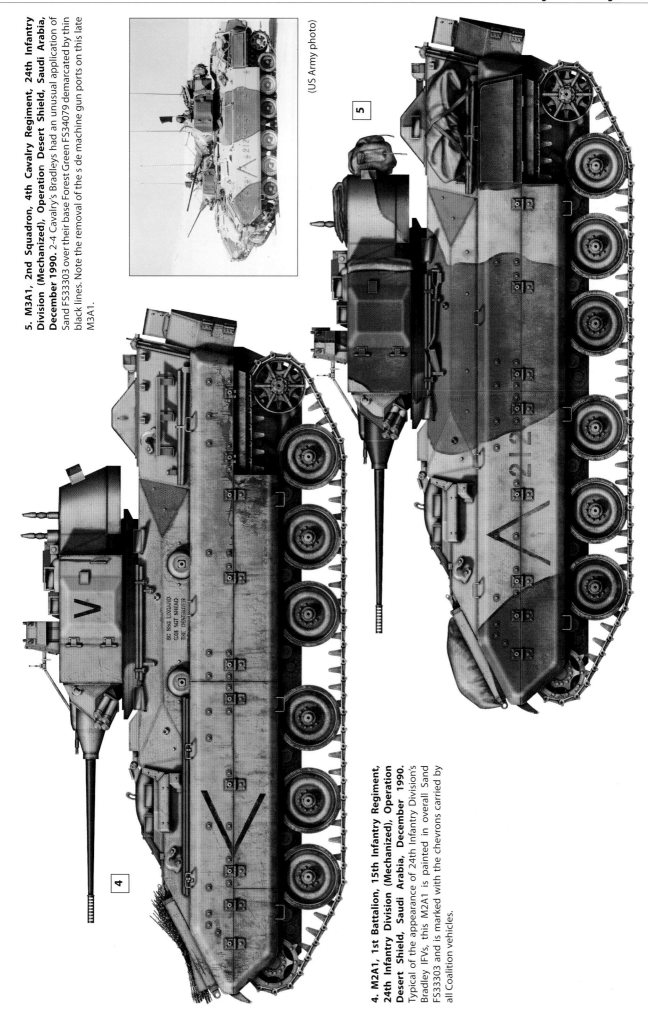

5. M3A1, 2nd Squadron, 4th Cavalry Regiment, 24th Infantry Division (Mechanized), Operation Desert Shield, Saudi Arabia, December 1990. 2-4 Cavalry's Bradleys had an unusual application of Sand FS33303 over their base Forest Green FS34079 demarcated by thin black lines. Note the removal of the s de machine gun ports on this late M3A1.

(US Army photo)

4. M2A1, 1st Battalion, 15th Infantry Regiment, 24th Infantry Division (Mechanized), Operation Desert Shield, Saudi Arabia, December 1990. Typical of the appearance of 24th Infantry Division's Bradley IFVs, this M2A1 is painted in overall Sand FS33303 and is marked with the chevrons carried by all Coalition vehicles.

6. M3A1, 3rd Squadron, 1st Cavalary Regiment, Fort Polk, LA, April 1990. This M3A1 has some interesting features. It has the internal configuration of a CFV but still has the hull roof periscopes of the M2A1 and the older-style rear stowage bin. It is painted in the new three-tone NATO camouflage of Green FS34094, Brown FS30051 and Black FS37030.

(US Army photo by Spc Diana Lindsey)

8. M2A2 ODS, 3rd Battalion, 15th Infantry Regiment, 3rd Infantry Division, Fort Stewart, GA, November 1997. This M2A2 ODS features the new-style driver's hatch and other ODS modifications, such as the turret roof-mounted GPS antenna. It has a solid coat of CARC Tan 686A FS FS33446.

7. M2A2, 1st Battalion, 23rd Infantry Regiment, 2nd Infantry Division, Exercise Foal Eagle 98, Twin Bridges Training Area, Republic of Korea, November 1998. This M2A2 is painted in the standard NATO camouflage of Green FS34094, Brown FS30051 and Black FS37030 and is fitted with the MILES 2 (Multiple Integrated Laser Engagement System) for simulating combat action during exercises.

9. **M2A3, 2nd Squadron, 5th Cavalry Regiment, 2nd Brigade Combat Team, 1st Cavalry Division, Operation Phantom Fury, Fallujah, Iraq, November 2004.** This IFV of the 'Lancers' squadron is finished in overall CARC Tan 686A FS FS33446.

9

(US Army photo by SSgt. Bronco Suzuki)

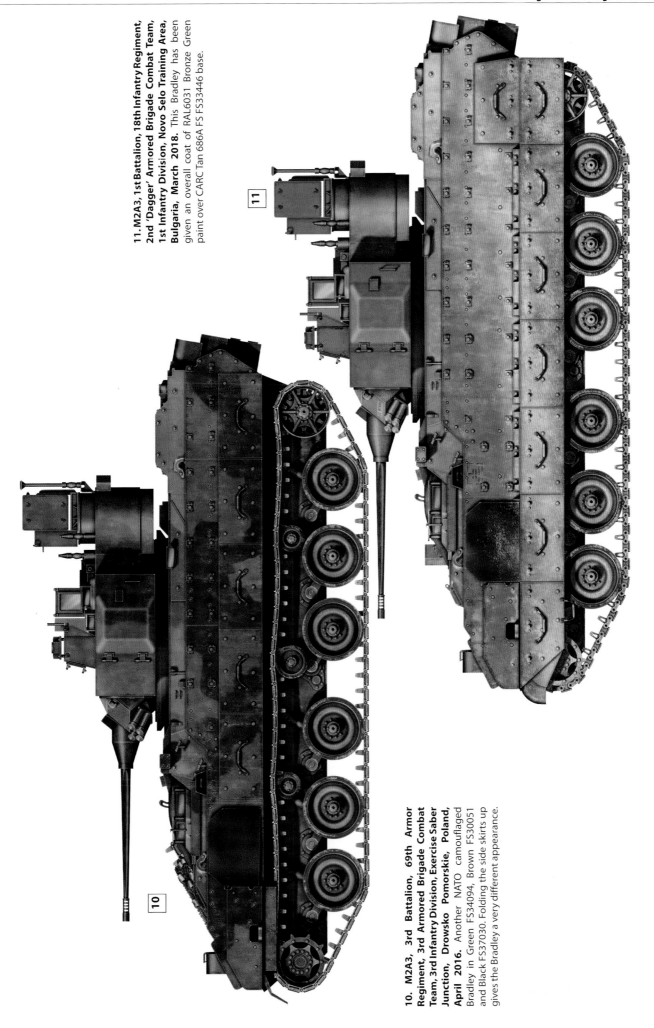

11. M2A3, 1st Battalion, 18th Infantry Regiment, 2nd 'Dagger' Armored Brigade Combat Team, 1st Infantry Division, Novo Selo Training Area, Bulgaria, March 2018. This Bradley has been given an overall coat of RAL6031 Bronze Green paint over CARC Tan 686A FS FS33446 base.

10. M2A3, 3rd Battalion, 69th Armor Regiment, 3rd Armored Brigade Combat Team, 3rd Infantry Division, Exercise Saber Junction, Drowsko Pomorskie, Poland, April 2016. Another NATO camouflaged Bradley in Green FS34094, Brown FS30051 and Black FS37030. Folding the side skirts up gives the Bradley a very different appearance.

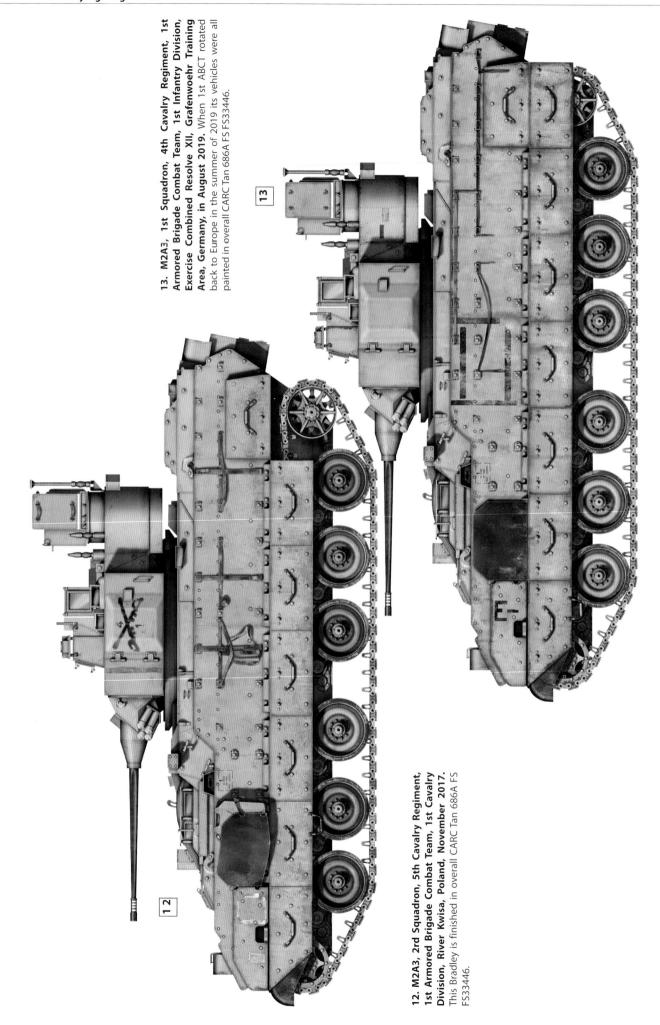

13. M2A3, 1st Squadron, 4th Cavalry Regiment, 1st Armored Brigade Combat Team, 1st Infantry Division, Exercise Combined Resolve XII, Grafenwoehr Training Area, Germany, in August 2019. When 1st ABCT rotated back to Europe in the summer of 2019 its vehicles were all painted in overall CARC Tan 686A FS FS33446.

12. M2A3, 2rd Squadron, 5th Cavalry Regiment, 1st Armored Brigade Combat Team, 1st Cavalry Division, River Kwisa, Poland, November 2017. This Bradley is finished in overall CARC Tan 686A FS FS33446.

M2
1-58 Infantry, 197th Infantry Brigade, Infantry Center, Fort Benning, GA 1983.
1/72, Trumpeter
David Grummitt

(right) The kit's running gear and tracks were replaced with the much better detailed resin items from OKB Grigorov.

(below) Trumpeter include a rudimentary interior largely based, it seems, on the 1/35-scale Tamiya M2.

(below right) The Winter Verdant MERDC (Mobility Research and Design Command) scheme consisting of Forest Green, Field Drab, Sand and Black was sprayed on freehand using Tamiya acrylics

(bottom right) An M2 fires down range at Fort Benning, GA, in June 1983. The four-colour Winter Verdant MERDC scheme is evident here. (US Army photo by Spc 5 Bobby Mathis)

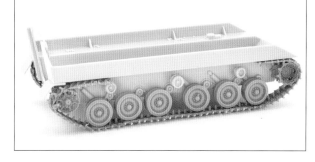

M2

1-7 Infantry,
3rd Brigade,
3rd Infantry Division,

Exercise
Central
Guardian,
Hesse, Germany,
January 1985.
1/35, Tamiya
David Grummitt

(below) Several improvements were made to the Tamiya kit, principally adding the anti-slip texture to the hull and adding several missing boltheads. The mounts for the deep wading screen were also added. The 25mm Bushmaster barrel is from RB Models.

(below) Some texture was added to the turret roof by stippling on Gunze's Mr Surfacer 1200.

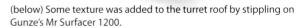

(above) A M2 IFV of 1-7 Infantry moves through the German village of Langgöns near Giessen during Exercise Central Guardian. (US Army photo by SSgt. Fernando Serna)

(below) The basic colours were laid down with Vallejo Model Air Forest Green (71.294), highlighted with Tank Light Green (71.044).

(below) The faded remnant of the winter whitewash was achieved with White over a coat of Vallejo's Chipping Medium (76.550).

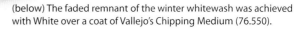

M3A1

2-4 Cavalry, 24th Infantry Division (Mechanized), Operation Desert Shield, Saudi Arabia, November 1990.

1/35, Tamiya

Torsten Wagner

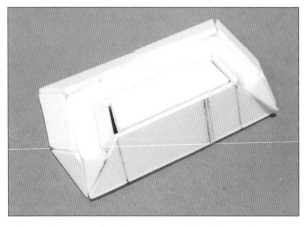

(above) A key piece of work was to scratch build the Cavalry Fighting Vehicle top hatch with vision blocks, as the Tamiya kit only has the Infantry Fighting Vehicle version.

(below) The missing shock absorbers and idler adjuster were scratch built from plastic rods and tubes.

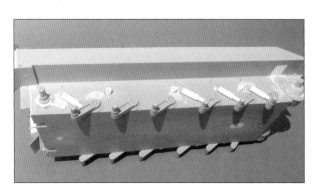

(above) The interior was heavily converted using parts from the Tamiya M2 kit. The additional TOW stowage on the right-hand side was scratch built.

(below) The turret interior was similarly scratch built with plasticard and detailed with copper wire.

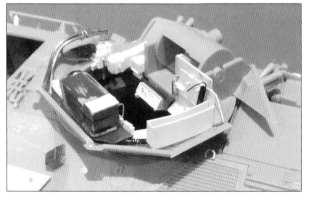

(above) The rear stowage lockers were rebuilt with plasticard and the ammunition box holders on the turret replaced with parts from the Meng Model Bradley.

(right) The side gun ports were completely covered with an additional armour plate on some M3A1s.

M2A2 ODS

Bravo Company, 1-26 Infantry, Task Force Falcon, 2nd Brigade Combat Team, 1st Armored Division, Kosovo, August 1999.

1/35, Tamiya
David Grummitt

(below) Tamiya's M2A2 ODS is a bit of a mish-mash, with several important features of the ODS Bradley missing. The most important of these is the driver's hatch, which is still the old style in the kit. It was replaced with the parts from a cannibalised Kinetic M3A3. Academy's kit does contain these and some other parts necessary to make an accurate M2A2 ODS.

(below) Another obvious omission is the anti-slip texture on the upper hull. This was added using VMS's excellent two-part solution. First, the required area is painted with the cement and the sand simply sprinkled on.

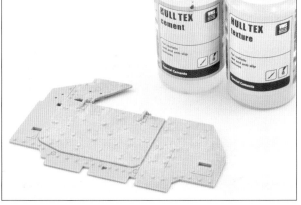

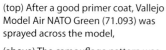

(top) After a good primer coat, Vallejo Model Air NATO Green (71.093) was sprayed across the model,

(above) The camouflage pattern was sprayed freehand, again using Vallejo acrylics (NATO Black 71.251 and NATO Brown 71.249). The model was weathered with oil paint washes and pigments.

(above right) A M2A2 of 2-2 Infantry takes up position on the Falcon 4 range near the town of Ramljane, Kosovo, in January 2003. Note the prominent KFOR marking on the appliqué armour and the KFOR bumper code. (US Army photo by Sgt. April Johnson)

M2A2 ODS
1-41 Infantry, 2nd Brigade, 82nd Airborne Division, As Samawah, Iraq, March 2003.
1/72, Dragon Models Limited
David Grummitt

(below) The fit of Dragon's Small-Scale Bradleys is excellent. The one-piece vinyl tracks are a little tight and need to be sewn together for a strong connection.

(below) The model was assembled out of the box save for the rear stowage which came from the Black Dog set (ref. T720006).

(below) Vallejo's US Modern Desert Colors (71.209) provides six Model Air paints perfect for airbrushing a 'modulated' finish on US Desert Storm or OIF AFVs. The idea is to start with the darkest shades then airbrush progressively lighter shades angling the airbrush over the model.

(above) Then the two middle shades are applied, achieving a gradual transition between the colours.

(above right) The two lightest shades provide the highlights. The lightest colour, Aged White (71.132), can also be applied by brush to certain raised details.

(right) After all the details and stowage has been painted, a pin wash using AK Interactive Wash for OIF & OEF (AK121) is applied to emphasise the fine detail on the Dragon kit.

A heavily stowed Bradley of 3rd Infantry Division in Baghdad in April 2003. (US Army photo by SSgt. Jeremy T. Lock)

M3A3 BUSK III

2-5 Cavalry, 2nd Brigade Combat Team, 1st Cavalry Division, Fallujah, Iraq, November 2004.
1/35, Meng Model
Patrick Winnepenninckx

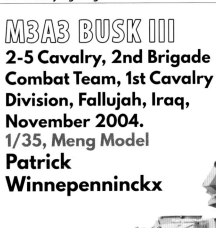

(below) Meng's Bradleys come with workable torsion bar suspension, ideal for diorama builders, which was fixed in place with superglue.

(below) The kit has nice anti-slip surfaces on the hull, but these were enhanced further with some putty dissolved in plastic cement.

(below right) Unlike their M2A3 kit, Meng's M3A3 doesn't include an interior, although they have released the M3 interior separately (kit ref. SPS-017).

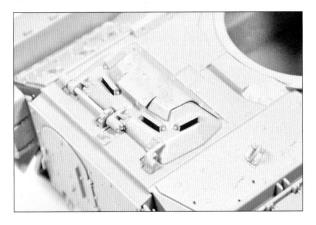

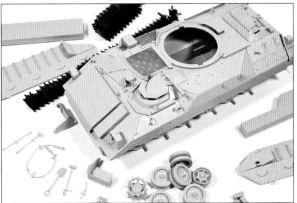

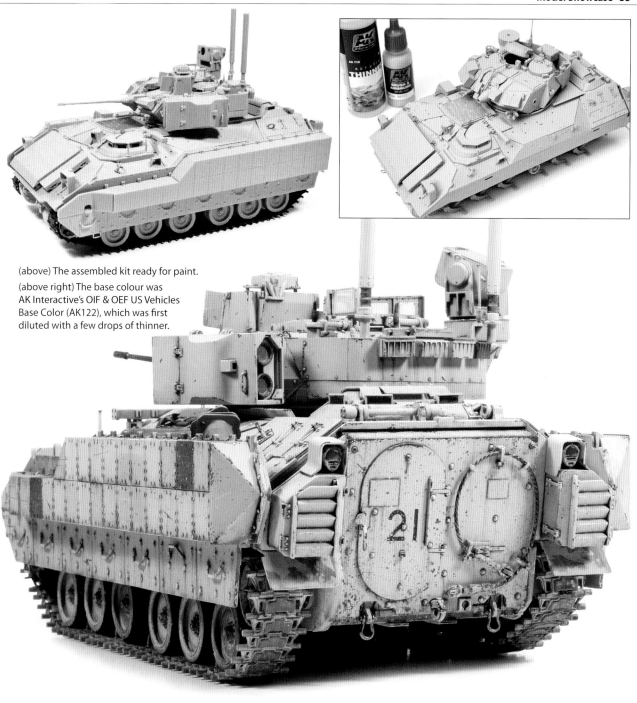

(above) The assembled kit ready for paint.

(above right) The base colour was AK Interactive's OIF & OEF US Vehicles Base Color (AK122), which was first diluted with a few drops of thinner.

An M3A3 from Apache Troop, 2-5 Cavalry, during the second battle of Fallujah in November 2004. (US Army photo by SFC Johancharles van Boers)

M2A3

**Alpha Company,
2-5 Cavalry,
1st Armored Brigade
Combat Team,
1st Cavalry Division,
Exercise Combined Resolve II,
Grafenwoehr Training Area, Germany,
June 2014.
1/35, Meng Model
Torsten Wagner**

(below) The most extensive additions were adding the MILES II gear, beacon and wiring to the turret. Good references are a must here.

(below right) A full interior was added and lit with LED lights for display when the rear ramp was down. Note too the X-161 tracks, available in Kinetic's M3A3 kit.

Meng's M2A3 is a great kit, but, like all plastic kits, it can always be improved with scratchbuilt and Aftermarket additions.

(below) The side armour and turret basket were scratchbuilt and detailed with Tamiya tape tie-down straps and the Eduard set for the Tamiya M2A2 ODS. Note the TOW launch simulator details added to the launcher assembly.

(below) M2A3s of 2-5 Cavalry take part in gunnery practice during Exercise Combined Resolve II. (US Army photo by 1st Lt. Aaron Shaffer)

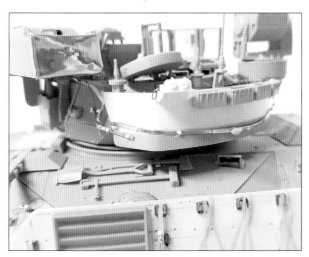

(left) Tamiya 35131
(above) Tamiya 35132
(below) Tamiya 35264

MODELLING PRODUCTS

The Bradley is a popular subject among modellers but has not been as well represented by the major kit manufacturers as you might expect. There is still a good variety of kits available, however, in both 1/35 and 1/72 scale and, with some work, they can be made to represent all the major production variants of the Bradley. In this section I have listed the various full kits of the Bradley Fighting Vehicle available, with some comments based on my own experience of building them and through speaking with other modellers. I've also listed most – but not all as some are long out of production – of the accessories and aftermarket details that can be used to enhance the appearance of a Bradley model.

FULL KITS: 1/35

The starting point for any discussion of the Bradley in miniature must begin with Tamiya's kit, first released in 1985. The kit was released in two versions: the M3 Bradley Cavalry Fighting Vehicle (ref. 35131) and M2 Bradley Infantry Fighting Vehicle (ref. 35132). The only difference between the two kits is that the M2 comes with a full interior, the side gun ports have the blanking off plate on the M3, and there are different decals for each. The kit is a pretty good representation of the M2/M3 and is basically sound in its dimensions. There are some simplifications and missing details, some more obvious and some more easy to remedy than others. The suspension is the most obvious oversimplification: the torsion bars are fixed in place and the shock absorbers and idler adjuster are completely absent.

(left)
Academy
13205

There is very little you do can to remedy this and there are no aftermarket sets currently available to replace the kit parts. The drive sprocket is also moulded as two complete halves, whereas the real thing had six lightening holes on the outer face. Finally, the drive sprocket mounts (B61 & 62) are incorrectly positioned and need rotating so the top is parallel to the upper hull. Looking across the upper hull there are numerous missing details, such as the lifting lugs on the exhaust plate and the circular mounts for the wading screen, but nothing that some good reference material can't fix. The other part of the Tamiya kit that is oversimplified is the armour around the rear access ramp. This requires some extensive surgery to correct and I suspect most modellers will be content to let this one lie.

Tamiya released an M2A2 (ref. 35152) in 1991 to coincide with the end of the First Gulf War. This was basically a re-release of the 1985 M2 kit containing an additional sprue with the new laminated armour side skirts. There are two major issues with these: first, they are provided as a single part when, of course, they are in reality two separate sheets; second, the left-hand plate is incorrectly shaped at the front with an odd protuberance (the box art for the M2A2 ODS kit shows the correct shape). The new sprue also contains the hull appliqué armour, new headlights and a new wading screen. The latter is incorrectly placed and would be better replaced altogether. Another thing to note is that neither the TOW launcher nor the early-pattern vinyl tracks have not been updated from the M2 kit. The final Tamiya release was of an M2A2 ODS (ref. 35264) which came out during Operation Iraqi Freedom. This contained another new sprue with OIF-era personal gear but didn't correct any of the outstanding issues with Tamiya Bradleys. Most notably it omitted some salient ODS features, such as the new-style driver's hatch and turret-mounted GPS aerial, but did have a new set of vinyl T-157 tracks.

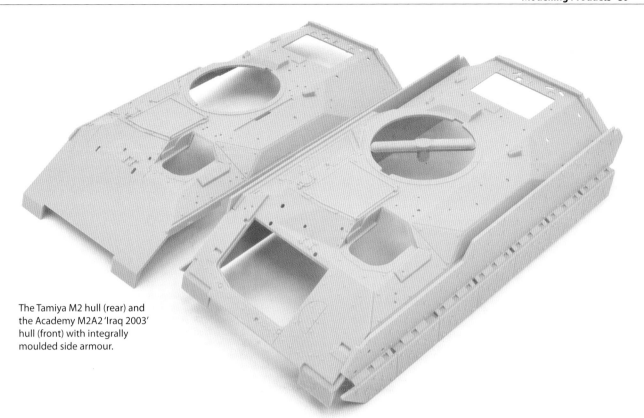

The Tamiya M2 hull (rear) and the Academy M2A2 'Iraq 2003' hull (front) with integrally moulded side armour.

Tamiya's Bradley was also the basis for Academy's kit, first released in 1985 in the M2 variant (ref. 048) and as an M3 two years later (ref. 050). This was an exact copy of the Tamiya kit and was reboxed several times by Academy and other Far Eastern manufacturers such as CC Lee and Hobbycraft. In 2006 Academy released their own M2A2 Bradley 'Iraq 2003' (ref. 13205). This is a much better starting point for an M2A2 ODS than the Tamiya one as it contains the correct ODS features, such as the new-style driver's hatch and turret-mounted GPS aerial. The hull is newly moulded with integral side skirts, although these still lack the obvious laminated appearance (but again this is relatively simple to fix).

In 2014 the Japanese company Orochi made a surprise entry into the market with a newly tooled M3A3 Bradley CFV. This came in two versions: a Deluxe Edition (ref. IM-001), which also included a turned brass barrel, resin figure, and a set of white metal T-157 tracks, and a Standard Edition (ref. IM-002), which didn't have the metal tracks or barrel. Both kits contained six crisply moulded sand yellow sprues, with a clear sprue, and two small frets of photoetch, while the Standard Edition had black plastic 'clickable' individual link tracks. The upper and lower hull came separately, with the former having the integrally moulded side skirts. This is a pretty good kit with a nicely detailed suspension immediately marking it as a different generation to the Tamiya and Academy kits. The kit also contained a full suite of hull Bradley Reactive Armor Tiles (BRAT), with optional bolts moulded onto the sprue that would need to be added if modelled without the BRAT. The TOW launcher and Commander's Independent Viewer are a little soft in detail, but still better than those offered in the Tamiya kits. The Deluxe Edition's extras are excellent. The Orochi T-157 tracks are superb with pre-cut tracks pins, as is the fluted metal barrel, although the inclusion of a resin explosive disposal officer is a little incongruous. The Orochi moulds were re-packaged in 2018 by Kinetic as M3A3 Bradley Fighting Vehicle (ref. 61014). This contains a new sprue containing some very nice link-and-length T-161 tracks, the only ones

available in 1/35 scale. The inclusion of the BRAT is anomalous, however, as no Bradleys fitted with T-161 tiles also sported the BRAT.

The same year as Orochi launched its M3A3, Meng Model released two versions of the Bradley: the M2A3 Bradley w/BUSK III (ref. SS-004) and M3A3 Bradley w/BUSK III (ref. SS-006). The two kits followed the Tamiya pattern in as much as the M2A3 contained a full interior, while the interior for the M3A3 was made available as a separate kit (ref. SPS-017). The Meng kits are superb kits to build, crisply moulded, well detailed and easy to assemble. Both kits come with working torsion bar suspension, nicely represented anti-slip texture, photoetched grills for the engine exhaust and, in the case of M2A3, a superbly detailed turret and fighting compartment interior, engine and transmission (the interior, engine and transmission are included in the separate kit for the M3A3). Individual link 'clickable' T-157 tracks are included, which are virtually identical to those in the Orochi Standard Edition kit. While well detailed, they are quite delicate once assembled. The Bradley Urban Survival Kit details come in the form of the BRAT and the Commander's Protection System. The M2A3 also includes the large rear air-conditioning units, although these are not

(below) Orochi IM-001

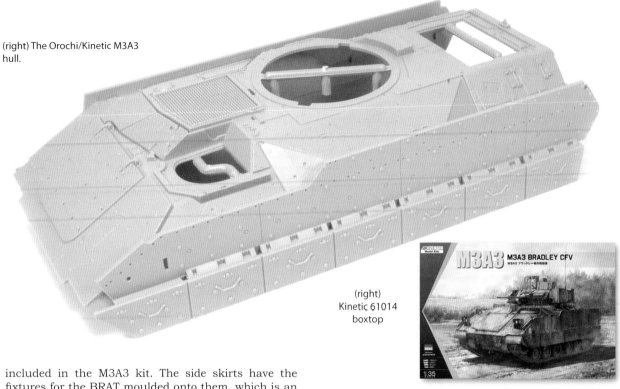

(right) The Orochi/Kinetic M3A3 hull.

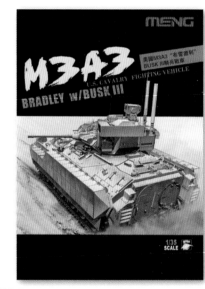

(right) Kinetic 61014 boxtop

(right) Meng Model SS-006 boxtop

included in the M3A3 kit. The side skirts have the fixtures for the BRAT moulded onto them, which is an issue if you want to build the M2A3/M3A3 without the BUSK. The only alternative is to scratch build the skirts or adapt the Tamiya M2A2 ones. The marking options given for the M2A3, including a vehicle for 2003, are a little suspect as the configuration of BUSK III certainly dates from the end of OIF or post-Iraq War, and the M3A3 markings are for CONUS vehicles from 2011 or 2014. The Meng kits are certainly the best detailed and most accurate 1/35-scale Bradleys, although the addition of the BUSK means that some thinking and a little conversion work will be necessary to depict the most commonly seen Bradley A3 configurations.

The author's build of the Kinetic Models' M3A3. Note the bolts that need adding in the BRAT is not fitted and the CIP from the Tamiya M2A2 ODS, not included in the Kinetic or Orochi kits.

FULL KITS: OTHER SCALES

In Quarterscale there aren't really any decent kits of the Bradley currently available. Zhengdefu made a poor motorised copy of the Tamiya kit back in the 1990s, which was subsequently reboxed by Kitech, but modellers wait for Tamiya to release the Bradley in

(above) Revell 03143

(below) Revell 03185

(right) The moulded-on driver's hatch is one of the big drawbacks of Revell's otherwise very good Bradley kits.

their 1/48-scale series as they have done for so many of their 1/35-scale kits.

In 1/72 scale the modeller is much better served by some very good kits of the Bradley. In 2001 Revell released a newly tooled M2A2 Bradley (ref. 03124). Revell were setting a standard for injection-moulded small-scale kits around this time and this is no exception. The kit came with five olive green plastic sprues and an attractive set of decals. The kit contains some very nice details, such as link-and-length tracks and a detailed multi-part TOW launcher assembly. The kit lacks the anti-slip texture, the properly laminated side skirts, and has some moulded-on tools, but this is excusable in this scale. Disappointingly, it also has a moulded on driver's hatch. In 2005 Revell released an M2/M3 kit (ref. 03143), which contained a new sprue with the M3 crew compartment hatch, early style side armour, and also two choices for the side firing ports on the first Bradleys. The kit contained decals for three Forest Green Bradleys seen in Germany during the 1980s. Revell re-released the M2A2 kit in 2011 (ref. 03185), with a new of decals and including the sprue for the M3 CFV, and the M2/M3 in 2017 (ref. 03143), again with new decals.

In 2004 Dragon Models Limited entered the fray with the first in an extensive line-up of small-scale Bradley kits. Their first was M2A2 ODS Bradley Iraq 2003 (ref. 7226). This kit represented a very specific vehicle, of 1-41 Infantry, shown on a photographic box top. It had the typical ODS Iraq War fittings, including turret-mounted GPS antenna, but still had the old-style driver's hatch. The kit is wonderfully detailed: two plastic sprues for the vehicle, as well as a separate upper and lower hull and turret, flexible 'DS' tracks, and a sprue of personal gear. The deep wading screen is also included in the kit, although not used, and there is also a CFV hull hatch and turret appliqué armour with the CIP. The kit has the level of detail you might expect from a 1/35-scale kit (the road wheels, for instance, come in separate halves with poly caps). The next release was a M3A2 ODS (ref. 7229), basically the same kit but with different vehicles for a USAEUR-based CFV. The third release was another M2A2 ODS OIF II Iraq 2004 (ref. 7247). This had a third set of markings, for 1-22 Infantry in Iraq in 2004, and also contained the large stowage basket seen on the side skirts. More importantly, this kit also contains the new-style driver's hatch. The next release, M2A2 w/ERA (ref. 7298), contained markings for four different IFVs fitted with the BRAT. This is a great kit, with the options given

(below) The link-and-length tracks included in the Revell Bradley kits.

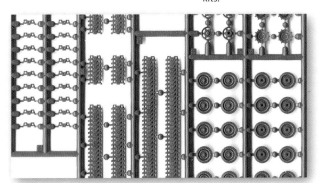

(below) Dragon 7226

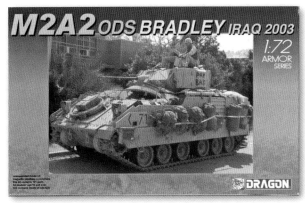

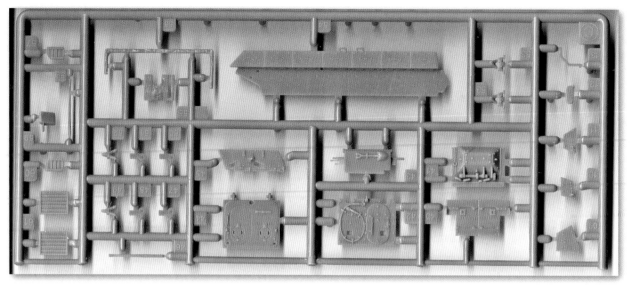

(above) The 'C' sprue contained in Dragon's range of excellent small-scale Bradley kits.

(above) Dragon 7298

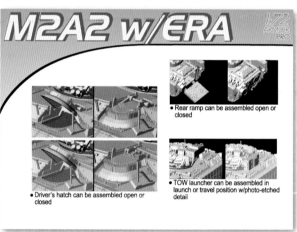

- Rear ramp can be assembled open or closed
- Driver's hatch can be assembled open or closed
- TOW launcher can be assembled in launch or travel position w/photo-etched detail

(above and below) Dragon 7298

(below Dragon 7324 - rereleased as 7623

- Extra armor plate on turret top
- CITV reproduced with slide-mold technology
- Turret bottom plate reproduced in great detail
- 'Doghouse' door can be assembled open or close
- GPS antenna added to bustle rack
- EPLR antenna base finely reproduced
- Extra armor around driver's hatch represents M2A3 Bradley
- OVM arrangement designed for M2A3 Bradley
- Rear ramp can be assembled open or closed
- New-looked backpacks realistically reproduced
- Photo-etched parts for ERA mounting frames
- One-piece track with crisp detail

11 11 · 11 11
73 73
4160 4160
A21 A21

www.dragon-models.com   e-mail: info@dragon-models.com   7623

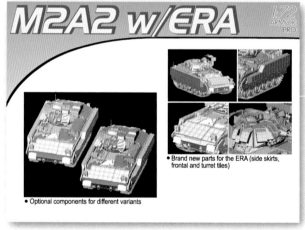

- Brand new parts for the ERA (side skirts, frontal and turret tiles)
- Optional components for different variants

for both the M2A2 and the M2A2 ODS and with some nice photoetched attachments for the turret BRAT. In 2007 Dragon released an M2A3 ODS (ref. 7324). This too is a superb kit. An additional sprue contains the Commander's Independent Viewer and extra turret top armour, as well as a retooled turret bottom with integral bustle rack and ammunition boxes. The turret and hull BRATs are also included as, as is the photoetch. M3A2 ODS Bradley w/ERA (ref. 7333) is a slimmed down boxing of the M2A2 ODS w/ERA kit, but without the M2A2 options. It does, however, contain a photoetched Commander's Protection System around the turret cupola. Markings are provided for a single OIF vehicle from 2-3 Cavalry. The final Bradley release by Dragon

(above) Dragon 7332

was the M6 Bradley Linebacker (ref. 7332), the only kit of this vehicle available in plastic. This contains a new sprue and some photoetch for the Stinger missile launcher and the newly tooled turret lower half. All of these kits are very difficult to find now, but thankfully Dragon have announced that they are re-releasing the M2A2 ODS w/ERA, the M3A2 ODS w/ERA, the M2A3 and M6 Linebacker kits in 2020.

Between 2008 and 2009 Chinese modelling giant Trumpeter released three small-scale Bradley kits. These are good kits but are, in fact, simply scaled-down versions of the Tamiya 1/35-scale kits, right down to the decal options. M2 Bradley (ref. 07295), like its Tamiya counterpart, contains a full interior. As you can see from the modelling gallery, it's a great little kit. The interior is also included in their M2A2 (ref. 07296) and M2A2 ODS/ODS-E (ref. 07297). The M2A2 ODS has the same issues as the Tamiya kit, but does include CIP and the later fluted gun barrel. For the price (about half that of the Dragon kits) Trumpeter's efforts are very good and a better option than the Revell ones.

There is little available in the way of small-scale resin kits of the Bradley. Polish firm Armo produced a M2 Bradley (ref. 72031) and an M2A2 (ref. 72032). More recently, Cromwell Models released an Armored Multi-Purpose Vehicle (ref. 72203) prototype based on the Bradley chassis.

(above) Trumpeter 07295
(above right) Trumpeter 07296

The separate driver's hatch and overall crispness of the moulding is evident in this image of Trumpeter's M2.

ACCESSORIES AND DETAIL SETS (1/35)

Given the variety of 1/35-scale Bradley kits available, there are relatively few details sets currently on the market. Eduard produced a range of very useful photoetch sets for the various iterations of the Tamiya and Academy kits, but these are no longer in production. They occasionally come up on eBay and some online vendors may still have them among their old stock. If you do get a chance to obtain one, do pick it up as there are some very useful replacement parts included. Blast Model also produced a resin track, wheel and suspension set for the Academy/Tamiya M2A2 (ref. BL35023K) but this too is now out of the production. In terms of replacement tracklinks currently available, AFV Club have both replacement vinyl (ref. AF35271) and individual link (ref. AF35133) T157 tracks. Friulmodel also produce some excellent single-link white metal tracks for early (ATL-78) and late-pattern T157 tracks (ref. ATL-79). Hobbyboss also produce plastic single-link tracks in the same patterns (refs. 81008, 81009). Spade Ace Models also produce individual link late-pattern T157 tracks (ref. SAT-35076). The best individual link T157 tracks available are without question the Orochi ones contained in M2/M3 Bradley Family Update Set (ref. PF-004). These are flawlessly cast and the box also includes pre-cut metal tracks pins and a very nice turned-brass 25mm Bushmaster cannon barrel.

There are several 25mm Bushmaster barrels available in 1/35 scale. Aber produce an early version (ref. 35L180), suitable for the M2/M3 up to some M2A2/M3A2 ODS vehicles, as do another Polish company, RB Model (ref. 35B15). Voyager produce an excellent fluted barrel for the Tamiya kit in their M2A2 Bradley Turret Weapon Set (ref. VBS0159). Voyager, in fact, currently produce the largest range of detail sets do the Bradley Fighting Vehicle. These include a

basic set (ref. PE35442), side skirts (ref. PE35443) and set of ERA tiles (ref. PE35470) for the Tamiya M2A2 ODS. There is also a set of Duke anti-IED antennas (ref. PEA273). Voyager also produce sets to enhance the detail on the Meng kits (refs. PE35660, PE35661, PE35371, PE35724, PE35725). For the advanced (or masochistic) modeller, they also provide a replacement set of photoetched ERA tiles. Photoetched detail sets for the Meng kits are also available from E.T. Model (refs. E35-218, E35-219 and E35-224) and Tetra Model Works (ME-35016, ME-35027). The Kinetic kit has been served by a new set from Eduard (ref. 36394), but this has little of use besides the engine and exhaust grills and if you do want a photoetched detail set for the Kinetic M3A3 the E.T. Model, Tetra Model Works or Voyager sets are a better bet.

In terms of accessory sets, the Bradley Stowage Set (ref. LF119) by Legend Productions contains a good range of suitable OIF-period stowage, although their resin conversion sets for the Tamiya kit have been superseded by the Meng kits. Verlinden Productions also offered a resin conversion, featuring ERA tiles, for the Tamiya kit (ref. 2182), now long out of production but equally superseded by the Meng kits. Eureka XXL produce a generic brass tow cable for the Bradley (ref. ER-3516), while Panzer Art produce a set of replacement resin roadwheels (ref. RE35-559). Two more manufacturers worth noting are the lenses and taillight sets produced by SKP (ref. 137 for Tamiya and ref. 279 for Meng Model), and the set of 3D-printed lights produced by FC Modeltrend (ref. 35702) for the Tamiya early M2/M3.

ACCESSORIES AND DETAIL SETS (1/72)

In small scale both Black Dog (ref. T72006) and CMK (ref. MV063) produce resin stowage sets for the Bradley. These are designed to represent OIF vehicles but can be

Orochi's detail set contains the best individual-link T157 tracks available in 1/35 scale, as well as an exquisite fluted 25mm Bushmaster barrel.

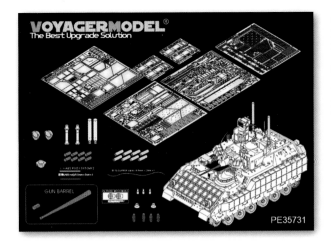

(above) Voyager's detail sets for the Meng Bradleys are typically complex multi-media affairs including photoetched brass, metal and resin parts.

(right) FC Modeltrend's 3D-printed replacement head and taillights for the Tamiya M2/M3 are a huge improvement on the kit parts but extremely fragile.

(below) The resin replacement roadwheels produced by the Bulgarian firm OKB Grigorov are much better than those offered in the Dragon, Revell or Trumpeter small-scale kits.

used for earlier vehicles. The Black Dog set is excellent as it provides a replacement rear stowage bustle for the Dragon kits, while CMK provides a better choice of suitable individual items. Two similar stowage sets are also offered by the Korean manufacturer Legend Productions (refs. LF7203, LF7205).

Probably the weakest part of all the small-scale Bradley kits are the tracks and replacement resin tracks are offered by both Model Miniature and OKB Grigorov. The Model Miniature set (ref. MM-R210) offers eight lengths of resin T157 tracks. OKB Grigorov offer both early and late-pattern wheels and tracks (refs. S72224, S72225, S72226, S72227). RB Model offer an excellent little brass replacement 25mm Bushmaster barrel (ref. 75B52), but at present there is no brass replacement option for the later fluted barrel. In terms of photoetched detail sets, Eduard and Polish manufacturer Part offer sets for the M2A2 ODS but these are now out of production, as are those made by Extraetch for the Revell kit. There was also a set of resin ERA by Verlinden Productions (ref. 2185), now out of production but also superseded by the excellent Dragon kit.

(above) An M270 MLRS during the Reforger '85 exercises. The similarities between the suspension and running gear of the Bradley and MLRS are clear in this image. (NARA)

OTHER BRADLEY VARIANTS

The Bradley Fighting Vehicle was from the outset considered as a basis for other AFVs and in June 1979 a third prototype was developed alongside the XM2 and XM3. The so-called Fighting Vehicle Systems Carrier (FVCS) eventually led to the Multiple Launch Rocket System (MLRS) which was first fielded in 1982, but of the other planned variants of the FVCS – an armoured logistics system, armoured maintenance vehicle, electronic fighting vehicle system, fire fighter and long range anti-tank program – only the XM4 Command and Control Vehicle was developed to full production. The M4 Command and Control Vehicle (2CV) finally entered service in 1997, designed to replace the aging M577A2 Command Post Vehicle, although only 25 were produced.

Variants of the Bradley itself are few in number, probably a reflection of the vehicle's unit cost and the versatility of the M113 which remains in US Army service. One area that the US Army has struggled with since the early days of the Cold War

is Short Range Air Defence (SHORAD). Early efforts to place Stinger MANPADS (Man-Portable Air Defence System) in the Bradley failed as the Stinger team had to dismount the vehicle to fire their missiles. The result of further development was the M6 Linebacker, an M2A2 ODS IFV with the TOW launcher removed and replaced with a launcher for four Stinger missiles. The M6 entered service in limited numbers and saw some action in the early stages of Operation Iraqi Freedom, but during 2005 and 2006 the vehicles were converted back to IFVs to meet the tactical needs of the Iraqi insurgency. In 2017 the SHORAD Bradley programme was restarted, but the US Army appear to favour a SHORAD capability based on the wheeled Stryker vehicle rather than the Bradley.

A more successful Bradley variant has been the M7 Bradley Fires Integration Support Vehicle (FIST-V). As early as the mid 1990s it was clear that the M113-based M981 FISTV was simply too slow to keep pace with the Armored Divisions' Abrams and Bradleys. By 1996 some

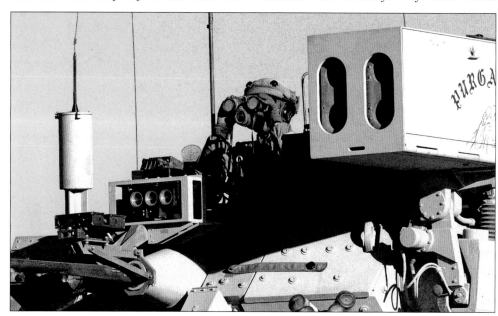

(right) A close-up of the launcher system of the M6 Linebacker of 1-22 Infantry during the Advanced Warfighting Experiment held at National Training Center, Fort Irwin, CA, in March 1997. (US Army photo by SSgt. William Cronk)

Two M2A3s of 1-63 Armor, 2nd Armored Brigade Combat Team, 1st Infantry Division on the Hohenfels Training Area during Exercise Combined Resolve X in May 2018. (US Army photo by Spc. Andrew McNeil)

Artillery Observers at the National Training Center had begun to convert the M3 CFV to the FISTV role. The current M7A3 are newly converted from M3A3s and serve in the Fires or artillery battalions of the Armored Brigade Combat Team The M7A3 is equipped with a targeting system that includes a Ground/Vehicle Laser Locator Designator (G/VLLD) and other electronic components in place of the TOW launcher.

As well as the M7A3, the Armored Brigade Combat Team is also equipped with the Bradley Engineer Squad Vehicle (ESV). These was originally converted from M2A2 ODS IFVs and carry the standard engineering equipment. They serve in the Brigade Engineer Battalion of the Armored Brigade Combat Team. In the USAEUR (United States Army Europe) the M3A2 also serves as an ESV.

One other Bradley variant is the Bradley Battle Command Post (BCP). Developed by BAE Systems, the BCP is designed to provide an armoured command and control post for the brigade and divisional commanders within the armoured forces of the US Army. It is based on the A3 standard Bradley and includes an enlarged rear area containing the necessary digital command and control equipment. The vehicle is still a prototype and no deliveries have yet been made to the US Army.

(below) A B-FISTV of 5-7 Cavalry at the National Training Center in February 2020. Note the Ground/Vehicle Laser Locator Designator instead of the TOW launcher and the two additional HF antennas at the rear of the vehicle. (US Army photo by Spc. Nathan Franco).

THE FUTURE OF THE BRADLEY

The changes made to the Bradley Fighting Vehicle since 2001 have largely been designed to make it better equipped to fight the kind of low-intensity conflicts in which the US Army was engaged in the wake of 9/11. The interim Bradley Urban Survivability Kit upgrades necessitated a comprehensive overhaul of the drive train and engine which formed a large part of the ECP I and II programmes and the resulting A4 standard Bradley Fighting Vehicle. However, the Russian annexation of Crimea and its intervention in the civil war in Ukraine from 2014 necessitated a major shift in the strategic planning of US military planners. Once more the possibility of a major war against a near-peer adversary became a priority and the principal warfighting systems of the US Armored Brigade Combat Teams – the Abrams MBT, the Bradley Fighting Vehicle and the M109 self-propelled howitzer – were required to adapt and evolve to meet the perceived new threat.

The changes planned for the Bradley are still under discussion, but a proposed new version would have replaced a planned third phase of ECP modifications and envisaged a new version, the Bradley Fighting Vehicle A5. Two significant changes, alongside a host of upgrades to existing systems, were under consideration. The first version would have had a larger hull, with the vehicle weight increased to some 40 tons and the capacity to carry an eight-man infantry squad. The second would see the Bradley up-gunned to carry the 30mm XM813 automatic cannon as currently fielded on the M1296 Stryker

Dragoon. When these changes were first seriously discussed, in 2018, there was some $600 million set aside in the US defence budget, but the future of the A5 project now seems less assured. The US Army decided to press ahead with its Next Generation Combat Vehicle (NGCV) family. This also included the BAE's Armored Multi-Purpose Vehicle (AMPV), the planned replacement for the M113. BAE Systems is also trialling its 'Black Knight' Unmanned Ground Combat Vehicle (UGCV), its first foray into unmanned, robotic military vehicle. These will comprise the new family of vehicles alongside the mobile Protected Firepower Light Tank and Optionally Manned Tank. In 2019 it was announced that the US Army would relaunch its prototyping competition for its Optionally Manned Fighting Vehicle (OMFV). However, only one bidder, General Dynamics Land System, entered the competition, with BAE Systems deciding not to submit a proposal, while another expected competitor, Raytheon and Rheinmetall, failed to deliver a bid sample. Therefore, in January 2020 the US Army decided to put its OMFV programme on hold for the time being. Congress also reduced the funding for the OMFV programme from $278 million to $173 million. The plan to have the precise specification for the Bradley replacement in place by 2023 and the first units equipped with the new vehicle three years later has clearly slipped. With these latest delays it seems the Bradley Fighting Vehicle will continue to be a mainstay of the US Army for some years to come.

(below) The Bradley continues to serve in the frontline: here an M2A3 of 1-6 Infantry, 2nd Armored Brigade Combat Team, 1st Infantry Division patrols in north-eastern Syria as part of Operation Inherent Resolve, the Coalition's attempt to defeat ISIS in Syria and Iraq, in September 2020. (US Army photo by SSgt. Michael West)

(left) A good view of the M242 25mm Bushmaster cannon on an early M2 IFV. Note the unprotected periscopes in the driver's hatch. (US Army photo by Spc 5 Bobby Mathis)

(centre) A close-up of the BRAT fitted to the hull and turret of an M3A2 ODS in Iraq in 2004. (US Army photo by Staff Sgt. Shane A. Cuomo)

(bottom left) A good view of the standard late-pattern T157 track fitted to the Bradley. The Bradley has 84 track links on the left side, but only 82 on the right. The tracks are steel with detachable rubber pads. They are the same as used on the United States Marine Corps' Assault Amphibious Vehicle (AAVP7). (US Army photo by Sgt. Patrick Eakin)

(below) These are the newer Extended Life T-161 tracks fitted to the M2A3 and M3A3 as part of the ECP I changes. (US Army photo by Sgt. Patrick Eakin)

(above) A good front-on view of an M3A3 during Exercise Combined Resolve in January 2020. Note the armoured glass protection around the commander's cupola and the prominent Driver's Vision Enhancer (DVE) in the centre of the hull, next to the driver's hatch. The DVE converts a thermal image to an adjustable image, allowing the driver to see a human figure at 400m at night or in adverse weather conditions. (US Army photo by Sgt. Megan Vander)

(above) A good view of the turret of the M7A3 B-FIST (Bradley-Fires Integration Support Team). Designed to allow the Forward Artillery Observer to keep up with the rest of the Armored Brigade Combat Team, the TOW launcher is replaced with a targeting system that includes a Ground/Vehicle Laser Locator Designator (G/VLLD) and other electronic components. (US Army photo by Spc. Matthew Marcellus)

Bradley Engineer Squad Vehicle, 82nd Engineer Battalion, 2nd Armored Brigade Combat Team, 1st Infantry Division, Grafenwoehr Training Area, Germany 2017. (Photos by Patrick Winnepenninckx)

(right) The Bradley ESV is based on an M2A3 IFV and can be fitted with a variety of engineering equipment. There are thirteen ESVs in the Brigade Engineer Battalion and the 2014 Table of Equipment states these should be M2A2 ODS, but the units rotated to Europe appear to have used pre-positioned M2A3s.

right) Here you can see the CIS of the M2A3 in a stowed position. Most of the vehicle is painted in a patchy coat of RAL 6031 Bronze over the CARC Tan 868. Note also the laminated armour plates of the side skirts.

(left) The ESV nearest the camera has the unit badge of an ox head, 'Babe the Blue Ox', on the TOW launcher housing.

(centre) A good view of the front of the vehicle, showing the large appliqué armour plates added to the hull from the A2 BFV onwards. Note the numerous attachment points for the ERA tiles.

(bottom left) In this image you can see the rough anti-slip texture applied to the hull front. The two fasteners at the top of the frontal hull armour plates are for a spare track link. Note to the patchily applied RAL 6031 paint.

(below) Note the heavy rubber mud guard and the armoured headlight covers fitted from the A2 onwards. Bradleys also have a rubber brush guard on the hull front behind which is carried a five-gallon water container.

(right) M2 IFVs operate alongside mechanised infantry during Exercise Central Guardian in January 1985. Central Guardian was conducted among freezing temperatures at the beginning, but a quick thaw at the end of January forced a premature end amid concerns of the damage that hundreds of armoured vehicle would inflict on the German countryside. (NARA)

THE BRADLEY IN SERVICE: COLD WAR WARRIOR

The Bradley Fighting Vehicle was, of course, designed to engage the massed armoured forces of the Warsaw Pact across the central German plain at the height of the Cold War. The first unit to be issued with the Bradley outside of the United States was 3rd Infantry Division, part of the United States Army Europe (USAEUR) and NATO's III (US) Corps. 3rd Infantry Division was also the first US Army division to move to the new Division 86 structure, part of the so-called 'Army of Excellence' programme. In the new Division 86 structure the M1 Abrams and M2 IFV replaced the M60A3 and M113 as the chief weapons systems of the armoured and mechanised infantry battalions. The H-Series Table of Equipment for the Division 86 armoured

division specified four rifle companies in each mechanised infantry battalion with thirteen Bradleys in each. Each battalion thus had 54 Bradleys (including the commander's and battalion training officer's vehicles). There were also six M3 CFVs in the battalion's reconnaissance platoon. Each Armored Division was to have four mechanised infantry battalions, while the Mechanized Infantry divisions had five. In 1986 the US Army's cavalry squadrons were also reorganised. Each cavalry squadron was originally to have two M3 CFV platoons and two M1 tank platoons, but this was deemed too costly and the tank platoons were removed from the Table of Organization. The transition to a heavy force equipped with Abrams and Bradleys was by no means complete by the end of the decade, however, and while most

(below) A German couple pass M2 IFVs of 1-7 Infantry, 3rd Brigade, 3rd Infantry Division, during Exercise Central Guardian on 24 January 1985. (US Army photo by SSgt. Fernando Serna)

of the units of USAEUR had transitioned to Abrams and Bradley by the end of the decade, some of the reserve divisions in the United States still had M60A3 and M60A1 MBTs and M113 APCs. Indeed, in 1990 five of the six Mechanized Infantry divisions and one Armored Division still retained cavalry squadrons with M60A1s and M113s.

While initial deliveries of the Bradley to frontline units were slow – by July 1984 only seventeen per cent of the 7,500 Bradleys procured were in service – their performance was impressive. They were first tried en masse during Exercise Certain Fury, part of the annual Reforger exercise held in September 1984. Bradleys from both the 2nd and 3rd Infantry Divisions took part in these field exercises. This led to an increasing realisation that the Mechanized Infantry, fighting in their Bradleys and keeping pace with the Abrams MBTs, would need to adopt different tactics to the traditional infantry ones of taking and holding ground. This was part of a wider change in US Army operational thinking known as the AirLand Battle, officially adopted in 1984. This envisaged the Abrams and Bradley, alongside Black Hawk and, from 1986, Apache helicopters and MLRS, aided by new command and control systems, carrying out a mobile, aggressive defence against any attacker. This was a strategy whose aim was 'not be simply to avert defeat – but rather it must be to win.' By the time of the large-scale Exercise Certain Strike, part of Reforger 87 in which 31,000 US troops were deployed to Germany from the United States, the Bradley equipped most of the frontline units of III (US) Corps and by the following year 4,919 Bradleys were in service throughout the US Army.

Despite its undoubted speed and firepower and its many advantages over the M113, these early deployments of the Bradley Fighting Vehicle were not without problems. Concerns in both the press and in Congress over the Bradley's aluminium armour have already been noted, but for the troops in the field the issues were more mundane and more immediate. The most pressing problems for the troops operating the new Bradley were failures of the transmission and malfunctions of the Integrated Sight Unit. In 1983 there were thirteen failed transmissions reported, with a further sixteen the following year. FMC introduced some modifications in 1985, which were rolled out to all new production vehicles two years later, and these reduced significantly problems with the transmissions. During Exercise Certain Strike less than one per cent of Bradleys broke down with transmission faults. Problems with the Integrated Sight Unit plagued Bradley units throughout the 'eighties, particularly issues with switching between high and low magnification. Of no less importance to the crew were issues with the crew compartment heater: during a two-week period in the winter of 1987 only one in 25 Bradley drivers in 3rd Infantry Division reported that the heater worked at all and some crews had resorted to operating their vehicles wrapped in sleeping bags! Of course, with the fall of the Berlin Wall in 1989 and the collapse of the Soviet Union two years later the strategic situation was transformed and the Cold War passed into history. The Bradley would, however, soon find itself engaged in a different theatre where its capabilities would become fully evident.

(below) An M3 CFV (note the blanked off firing ports in the hull side) rides at speed through a German town during Exercise Central Guardian. (NARA)

OPERATION DESERT STORM

As the Cold War in Europe drew to its conclusion, the Bradley Fighting Vehicle found itself engaged in a very different theatre but one in which the traditional roles of armour and cavalry would come to the fore. On 2 August 1990 Iraqi forces invaded Kuwait. Within 48 hours the Emir had fled, the Kuwaiti armed forces had either surrendered or escaped to Saudi Arabia, and a coalition of nations, led by the United States, was organising to demand the Iraqis withdraw from what Saddam Hussein would soon declare 'the nineteenth province of Iraq'. The invasion had been planned long in advance and the warning signs largely ignored by the Kuwaitis and their allies. At the time Iraq had the fourth largest army in the world and their soldiers had recent combat experience in the long and bloody Iran-Iraq War, which had ended just two years previously. Nevertheless, by the end of February 1991 the Iraqi army had been effectively destroyed and the invaders had been thrown out of Kuwait in ignominious defeat. The ground campaign, which lasted just one hundred hours, would prove the effectiveness of the Bradley both as an armoured fighting vehicle and as an integral component of the US Army's warfighting capability.

In the aftermath of the Iraqi invasion of Kuwait the US quickly reinforced Saudi Arabia with armour. The first US tanks deployed to the Gulf were the forty M551 Sheridans of 82nd Airborne Division, which arrived in Saudi Arabia on 7 August. By the beginning of September, the first M1 Abrams of 24th Infantry Division (Mechanized) had arrived in theatre, followed by 1st Cavalry Division, the 1st 'Tiger' Brigade of 2nd Armored Division and the 3rd Armored Cavalry Regiment. By the end of November 1990 the United States had deployed 760 M1/M1A1 Abrams and 610 M2/M3 Bradley Fighting Vehicles. The build-up of armoured forces continued into the New Year with the arrival of elements of 1st and 3rd Armored Divisions, 2nd Armored Cavalry Regiment, 2nd and 5th Marine Expeditionary Force, the 5th Marine Expeditionary Brigade and various other units. By the time the 15 January deadline for Iraqi forces to leave Kuwait had expired, the United States had deployed nearly 2,000 Abrams (mainly the new 120mm-armed M1A1), some 300 M60s and 2,200 Bradleys to Saudi Arabia. These included 834 of the new A2 standard Bradleys shipped from POMCUS (Prepositioning of Equipment Configured in Unit Sets) depots in Germany and direct from the production line at FMC in San Jose, CA.

At the start of the ground campaign, then, the frontline US Army units deployed 1,730 Bradleys of all three types, with 470 held in reserve. The 24th Infantry Division (Mechanized), serving on the eastern flank with XVIII Airborne Corps, was equipped with M2A1, while 3rd Armored Cavalry Regiment had the newer M3A2. 1st Armored Division, serving in the centre with VII Corps was largely equipped with M2A2 and M3A2, while the other armoured division in the Corps, 3rd Armored Division, was equipped with the older A1 variants. 1st Infantry Division, which faced the Breach Zone, in VII Corps' area of responsibility still had M2A0 IFVs, although its cavalry squadron, 1-4 Cavalry, had M3A2s. The two brigades of 1st Cavalry Division assigned to VII Corps were similarly equipped with M3A2s, as was the 2nd Armored Cavalry Regiment. This was the largest concentration of American armour assembled since the end of World War II and it required a massive logistic effort. The experience of moving men and material to Europe as part of the annual Reforger exercises was vital, but concerns remained, particularly

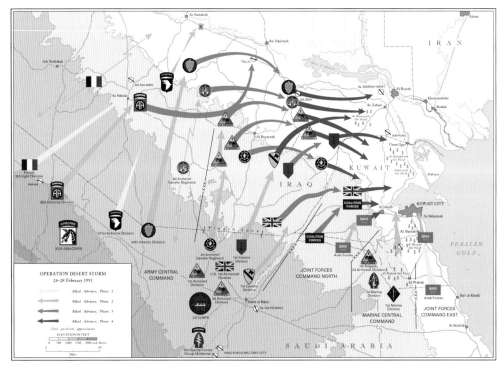

(right) The Coalition forces had assembled an unprecedented array of armoured firepower against the Iraqi forces in southern Iraq and Kuwait for Operation Desert Storm in February 1991. (Jeff Dahl)

(left) An M2A1 of 1-15 Infantry, 24th Infantry Division (Mechanized) in the Saudi desert during Operation Desert Shield. (US Army photo by Sgt. Brian Cumper)

over shortages of the new M919 depleted uranium Armour Piercing, Fin Stabilised Discarding Sabot, Tracer (APFSDS-T) round for the 25mm cannon. Some three million 25mm rounds were transported to the Gulf, but the armour-piercing M919 round had only entered production the year before and supplies were limited. In the event, as we shall see, these shortages proved no obstacle to the Bradley's success in engaging and destroying Iraqi armour.

Indeed, it is generally acknowledged that more Iraqi AFVs were destroyed by Bradleys than by Abrams MBTs. The new M1919 proved deadly against the lightly armoured Iraqi BMP-1s and MTLBs. It was estimated that Bradley gunners fired only six 25mm rounds for each enemy AFV destroyed. The M919 was also effective against the side armour of older Iraqi tanks, such as the Chinese-build Type 59 and soon became the weapon of choice for Bradley gunners. 3rd Armored Division, for example, expended 10,214 rounds of 25mm ammunition, but fired only 101 TOW missiles. The TOW's effectiveness in the difficult visibility of the ground campaign was hampered by the lack of a laser rangefinder, yet Bradleys were still able to destroy enemy tanks at ranges of up to 3,700 metres. Fears about the Bradley's survivability remained largely unfounded. Only three Bradleys were completely destroyed by enemy fire, while seventeen were lost to friendly fire, mostly from M1A1 hits as a result of the chaos of battle. A further twelve Bradleys were damaged, three by friendly fire incidents.

Such statistics shouldn't hide the hard fighting that the Bradley crews were subjected to. During the battle of 73 Easting, Ghost Troop, 2nd Armored Cavalry Regiment arrayed its nine M1A1 MBTs and twelve M3A2 CFVs against elements of the Iraqi Republican Guard's 3rd Tawakalna ala-Allah Mechanised Division. By mid-afternoon on 26 February the troop was

aware that its neighbouring troops were all engaged against dug-in Iraqi positions. The troop commander, Captain Joseph Sartiano, threw his tanks forward in a reversal of the usual tactics and advanced to contact with the enemy. Before long they were engaged in a heavy firefight with an enemy they could not see amidst a ferocious sandstorm. "This is total chaos" remarked one Bradley driver into the tape recorder he had recording in his vehicle. Then the crew of Bradley G-16 reported enemy infantry to their front at close range. Their coaxial machine gun had jammed and they radioed the other Bradleys in their platoon to try and ascertain what was going on. There was a large explosion nearby, followed by as second even closer: "it was like somebody hit us with a sledgehammer" said the driver Spc. Patrick Bledsoe. The Bradley's gunner was dead and its commander wounded, victims of an Iraqi T-55 which was then destroyed by the troop commander's M1A1. As the sandstorm worsened, the Iraqis increased their efforts to destroy Ghost Troop. By 18:00 the troop had nine destroyed Iraqi AFVs to their front for the loss of one Bradley. Waves of Iraqi infantry came against the Bradleys and were killed by fire from the 25mm cannon and coaxial 7.62mm machine gun. The troop commander requested air support, but none was available. In the end concentrated American artillery fire, called in by the Bradley platoon commander who had to leave his vehicle and crawl to the Forward Artillery Observers because the radios were too busy, broke the Iraqi assault. In fact, after debriefing captured Iraqi officers, it transpired that two Iraqi units, the Tawakalna and 12th Armoured Divisions, had been trying to retreat along the same route and had come across Ghost Troop by accident. In 100 hours of ground combat 2nd Armored Cavalry Regiment destroyed a hundred Iraqi tanks, about fifty

APCs and numerous artillery pieces. Some 90 per cent of those, the equivalent of an entire Iraqi brigade, were destroyed during the battle of 73 Easting.

Ghost Troop's experience, and the tenacity of the Iraqis they faced, was not typical of US armoured units during the ground war, but every Bradley unit was impressed by the performance of their vehicle. 4-7 Cavalry, 3rd Armored Division, was also engaged against Republican Guard units at Medina Ridge. Here the M3A1 Bradleys were organised into mechanized scout platoons each of six CFVs. A Troop lost two Bradleys completely destroyed and two men dead, but in after battle reports they stated that their Bradleys had survived numerous hits from Iraqi tank guns. One Bradley took an RPG round and two sabot rounds from a T-72 tank without the loss of any of its crew. The fire suppression systems in the Bradley worked well and the crew suffered only minor flash burns or shrapnel hits. The damage the Bradleys of A Troop inflicted upon the enemy was severe. The platoon sergeant recalled: "Our main guns blew up every BMP they fired at, and our TOW missiles destroyed every tank they hit. We had ten out of eleven hits with the TOW". The cavalrymen considered the Bradley too large a vehicle with which to scout effectively and complained that all eighteen of the Troop's coaxial machine guns jammed but concluded that "it's an awesome weapon when you have to go toe-to-toe with enemy armor."

In January 1992 an early performance assessment on the Bradley and Abrams during Operation Desert Storm was submitted to the House of Representatives. It considered five parameters to judge the performance of the US Army's two principal warfighting systems: reliability, survivability, lethality, mobility and range. The reliability of the Bradley was considered to between 92 and 96 percent for the A2 variants and 89 to 92 percent for the older vehicles during the combat phase. Its survivability and mobility, especially in the newer A2 variant, was considered excellent and, as we have seen, both the 25mm cannon and TOW launcher proved themselves deadly weapons. The range of the Bradley was impressive, much better than that of the Abrams: 2nd Armored Cavalry Regiment travelled 120 miles in eight hours without the need to refuel. Crews did report a number of minor issues, including leaking radiators, unreliable heaters and misdirected exhausts, as well as a tendency for the co-axial machine gun to jam, but none of these compromised the ultimate effectiveness of the Bradley. Several crews, however, noted that the Bradley's lack of speed in reverse placed it at a disadvantage compared to the Abrams. The lack of a laser rangefinder was again noted, as was the urgent need for a friend-or-foe identification system to avoid the 'blue-on-blue' incidents that had dogged the Coalition forces throughout the ground campaign. Concerns were also raised about the effectiveness of the Army's communications network and the need for a navigation system. More worryingly perhaps for the future, was the inability of the Army's supply train to keep pace with the fast-moving Abrams and Bradleys. 1st Cavalry Division reported that 60 per cent of its store of spare parts were exhausted by the end of the campaign. The pace of the Bradleys' and Abrams' advance was also an issue for the other vehicles in the combat units, such as the M109 self-propelled howitzer and the various vehicles based on the M113 APC. Many of these concerns were addressed in the A2 ODS version of the Bradley, but Operation Desert Storm was a resounding triumph for the Bradley Fighting Vehicle and the concept of fast-moving, aggressive armoured warfare it represented.

(right) Another 1-15 Infantry M2A1 during Operation Desert Shield. The enormous amount of supplies required to keep the armoured units in the field is evident from the material at this temporary shelter. (US Army photo by Sgt. Brian Cumper)

(left) An M2A2 of 4-12 Infantry, Task Force Eagle, enters a patrol base in Bosnia in April 1996. Note the prominent IFOR marking carried on the rear of the turret stowage basket. (US Army photo by SSgt. Andy Dunaway)

BOSNIA AND KOSOVO

In the 1990s the Bradley Fighting Vehicle played a key role in the United States' and NATO's ability to project force in a series of missions with a peacekeeping, or peace-enforcing, mandate. In 1993, in the immediate aftermath of the disastrous battle of Mogadishu, where nineteen US soldiers were killed by Somali militiamen, a Bradley company belonging to 24th Infantry Division (Mechanized), with an attached platoon of M1A1 Abrams, was despatched to protect US interests. Their intervention was short-lived and the new Clinton administration soon made the decision to withdraw US forces from the country.

The US involvement as part of the NATO missions to Bosnia and Kosovo were, however, on a different scale altogether. In early 1992 war broke out in the newly independent state of Bosnia-Herzegovina between the Bosniaks, the mainly Muslim, Bosnian-speaking native of Bosnia-Herzegovina, and their ethnic Serbian and Croatian neighbours, who claimed part of the territories of the nascent state for themselves. In February 1994 the United States brokered a peace between the Bosniaks and the Bosnian Croats. The ethnic cleansing by the Serbs continued apace, however, and by the middle of that year half a million Bosnian Muslims had been displaced. In April NATO launched its first airstrikes against Bosnian Serb targets, while the Bosnian Serbs ambushed a Danish UNPROFOR contingent. NATO airstrikes intensified into 1995, but in July of that year one of the worst atrocities of the conflict occurred when some 8,000 Bosniaks were murdered by Bosnian

Serbs at Srebrenica in eastern Bosnia. In December the presidents of Bosnia, Croatia and Serbia signed the Dayton Peace Accords, bringing an end to three-and-a-half years of vicious war in Bosnia. NATO's response was the deployment of IFOR (Implementation Force), a force of some 60,000 personnel organised into three multi-national divisions, to implement the agreement and protect the Bosnian civilian population from Serbian sectarian violence.

The US Army took command of Multi-National Division North (MNDN), one of three such divisions deployed to Bosnia, with its base at the former Yugoslav airforce base at Tuzla, renamed Camp Eagle. As well US forces deployed on 2 December 1995 as 'Task Force Eagle'. Under the command of 1st Armored Division and divided into two Brigade Combat Teams, the Abrams, Bradleys and other AFVs of 1-1 Cavalry, 3-4 Cavalry, 3-5 Cavalry, 4-67 Armor, 2-68 Armor and 4-12 Infantry moved from their bases in Germany by train through Hungary and Croatia to Bosnia. The final leg of the journey was to cross a pontoon bridge spanning the River Sava into Bosnia. On Christmas Day 1995 the M3A2 Bradleys of A Troop, 1-1 Cavalry were the first unit to cross the Sava and secured the bridgehead. A second bridge over the Sava was completed on 17 January 1996. As one American officer observed: "The task force deployed with sufficient force to annihilate the factional armies. Clearly, this was instrumental in ensuring their full cooperation and compliance."

The difficult terrain took its toll on the US Armor. 1-1 Cavalry, for instance, deployed to Bosnia with 39 M3A2 Bradleys and twelve M1A1 Abrams. Within six months

1-1 Cavalry's vehicles were more or less worn out, patrolling thousands of miles through Bosnia's fragile road network and the narrow streets of its town and villages. On several occasions 1-1 Cavalry earned the ire of local residents as the Abrams and Bradleys ripped the doors off parked cars or destroyed already poor road surfaces by executing on the spot turns. Somewhat controversially 1-1 Cavalry exchanged its Bradleys for the new up-armoured HMMWV, the XM-1114. This, it was argued, both saved money and allowed the scouts to be much more versatile in their peacekeeping mission. As IFOR's mission and Operation Joint Endeavour ended and a new mission (Operation Joint Guard) began with the transition to a Stablisation Force (SFOR) on 20 December 1996, the case for the up-armoured HMMWV to take over the scout role seemed compelling. Others argued, however, that the safety of U.S. troops was being put at risk by a cost-cutting exercise, a claim that seemed to be borne out in September 1997 when an XM-1114 was almost overturned in the town of Brčko with its crew inside it during riots preceding the Bosnian elections.

If the NATO intervention in Bosnia was a peace-keeping mission, designed to keep the warring ethnic groups apart and implement a peace settlement, the Alliance faced a much more difficult and dangerous mission three years later in Kosovo. In the summer of 1998 activities by the Kosovo Liberation Army (KLA) led to reprisals by the Yugoslavian and Serbian military, largely aimed against Kosovo's Albanian Muslim population. In October NATO launched limited airstrikes against Yugoslav targets, but the fighting in Kosovo, and the atrocities, intensified. The failure of peace talks led to a much more sustained and intense NATO air campaign, which lasted from March until June 1999. On 10 June NATO suspended its air campaign when Yugoslavia agreed to withdraw from Kosovo and two days later

NATO's Kosovo Force arrived to separate the warring parties and enforce peace in Operation Joint Guardian.

The first US unit to enter the country, on 13 June, was a taskforce 2-505th Airborne, 82nd Airborne Division, including the Abrams of Company C, 1-35 Armor and Bradleys of Company D, 1-16 Infantry, 1st Armored Division. The armour flew into Macedonia from Albania from where they carried out a road march into Kosovo, establishing Camp Bondsteel the town of Kacamik as the main base of Task Force Hawk. In Kosovo the Bradleys operated patrols alongside the Abrams, as well as other members of the multi-national NATO force, especially the Poles of 18th Airborne Battalion. On 5 July Bradleys and Abrams of 1-77 Armor and 1-26 Infantry, 2nd Brigade Combat Team, 1st Infantry Division, part of Task Force Falcon, also entered the country. 1-26 Infantry deployed with the new M2A2 ODS, the first unit in USAEUR to receive it. Once they had secured the south-east corner of the country, the mission was principally to prevent illegal arms smuggling across the border. It was not without casualties and 1-26 Infantry lost two men killed in action on 17 July and a third on 9 August.

Bradleys continued to be deployed as part of NATO's mission to Kosovo up until Operation Iraqi Freedom demanded the participation of the US Army's armour in a new theatre. The deployments to the Balkans were a formative episode in the history of modern American armoured force. While some questioned the place of heavy armour in the future wars American planners imagined, to the men on the ground the Abrams and the Bradleys were very welcome, saving lives and being the ultimate expression of US military power. Moreover, the valuable operational experience gained in the Balkans would stand the tanks and mechanised infantry in good stead during the war in Iraq.

(right) The commander of an M2A2 ODS of Charlie Company, 3-7 Infantry, 3rd Infantry Division, Task Force Falcon, scans the horizon from White Base, Outpost 1, near the village of Mucibaba, Kosovo, in May 2001. (US Army photo by SSgt. Bronco A. Suzuki).

THE IRAQ WAR

On 20 March 2003 some 130,000 US soldiers, assisted by 45,000 troops from the United Kingdom, and smaller numbers from Australia and Poland, invaded Iraq. The initial offensive lasted just 41 days and on 1 May President George W. Bush announced "mission completed." Yet before long the invasion had deteriorated into a long and bloody insurgency which would not end even with the withdrawal of US forces in 2011. During this long war, which cost 4,400 American lives and some $478 billion, the Bradley Fighting Vehicle played an important part and its role changed throughout the war reflecting its versatility and the adaptability of the men who served in it.

For the initial invasion the US Army's Bradleys and Abrams were concentrated in Lieutenant General Wallace's V Corps. This was comprised of the armour, cavalry and mechanised infantry regiments of 3rd Infantry Division and 4th Infantry Division, while 1-41 Infantry, detached from 1st Armored Division, served with the 2nd Brigade of the 82nd Airborne Division. Early in the campaign the Americans were keen to avoid the kind of urban fighting that had relatively recently proved so disastrous for the Russians in Grozny during the First Chechen War. Instead the Americans conceived of a 'Thunder Run' into Baghdad, a massive armoured raid into the heart of the Iraqi capital designed to induce a sense of imminent defeat and the collapse of Iraqi resistance. On 5 April a battalion-sized taskforce of 1-64 Armor, 2nd Brigade, 3rd Infantry Division, spearheaded by thirty M1A1 Abrams and fifteen M3A2 Bradley CFVs, passed along the west bank of the

Tigris River into the heart of the Iraqi capital. By midday 1-64 Armor had left the centre of Baghdad leaving some 2,000 Iraqi dead for the loss of a single Abrams to an RPG (Rocket-Propelled Grenade) hit. The success of the first 'Thunder Run' led two days later to a second brigade-sized mission to seize the centre of Baghdad and its government buildings. The Iraqis had fortified the routes into Baghdad, yet it had no effect on the American advance and within a few hours of the Bradleys and Abrams of 2nd Brigade had secured the centre of the city, including the Republican Palace Complex and Ba'ath Party headquarters. The 'Thunder Runs' exploited the speed and survivability of the both the Abrams and Bradley. The scouts and mechanised infantry remained in their vehicles and the Iraqis had no opportunity to engage the American soldiers who refused to engage in the street fighting that had previously characterised urban operations. 2nd Brigade's operations succeeded as well because of the training and discipline of the US forces and the flexibility afforded to the units to make tactical decisions on the ground.

Elsewhere during the invasion of Iraq the Bradley proved its worth. In the north of the country the 173rd Airborne Brigade, which had parachuted into Bashur Airfield were slowed in their advance to Kirkuk until they were joined by the Abrams and Bradleys of 1-63 Armor, 3rd Brigade, 1st Infantry Division. 1-63 Armor was part of the USAEUR's Immediate Ready Task Force, a heavy force that had been maintained in Germany since the NATO intervention in Kosovo in 1999. The force included a Heavy Ready Company comprised of one M1A1 Abrams platoon and one M2A2 ODS

(above) An M2A2 ODS of 2-130 Infantry, 3rd Brigade, 3rd Infantry Division on patrol bear Baqubah, north of Baghdad, in April 2005. 130th Infantry Regiment is part of the Illinois National Guard and was one of several Guard units that served in Operation Iraqi Freedom. (US Army photo by SSgt. Eddie L. Bradley)

IFV platoon with two additional platoons of M113A3s. The Abrams and Bradleys of 1-63 Armor were flown into Bashur Airfield on 8 April. Two days later, with Kurdish Peshmerga forces pressing the Iraqi army hard in Kirkuk and Irbil, the commander of 173rd Airborne Brigade decided to throw his limited armoured forces forward towards Irbil in a mini 'Thunder Run'. Again, the psychological effect of heavy armour, both on the Iraqi army and the local Kurdish populace, was immense, but without the necessary logistics and mechanical support Task Force 1-63 Armor was unable to press ahead at once towards Kirkuk. Eventually TF 1-63 Armor continued its advance was instrumental in allowing 173rd Airborne Brigade to secure the vitally important Kirkuk airfields. TF 1-63 Armor showed the ability of the Bradley to be airlifted to a remote battlefield in support of light infantry and special forces and make an immediate impact. As one Special Operations soldier observed: "we have done all that we can do. We've bombed these guys for three weeks. We need tanks and heavy infantry to drive them off the ridge."

The Bradley Fighting Vehicle again proved its worth during the second battle of Fallujah during November and December 2004. 2-7 Cavalry fought alongside the United Marine Corps as part of Regimental Combat Team 1 in the west of the city, while 2-2 Infantry (Mechanized) served as part of the Regimental Combat Team 7 in the east. Small groups of buttoned-up Abrams and M2A3s drove through the city subduing the insurgents with their firepower. Earlier the same year the so-called 'Baghdad Box'

formation had been used to effect against the Shia militias in Sadr City. Interviews with the ten Bradley battalions that had participated in Operation Iraqi Freedom up to the end of 2004 revealed a generally positive view of the vehicle's contribution. The Bradley Reactive Armor Tiles (BRAT) in particular proved very effective in protecting the vehicle and its crew against RPG attacks and only three Bradleys were lost of enemy action. The firepower of the 25mm Bushmaster cannon was intimidating and often enough to deter insurgent attacks. The greatest success, however, was the superb situational awareness of the Improved Bradley Acquisition Sub-System (IBAS) and the Commander's Independent Viewer (CIV) on the A3 variant. These allowed the Bradley to move buttoned-up through urban areas deploying maximum firepower with maximum survivability. The survivability of the Bradley was such that some units, such as 2-69 Armor, replaced the HMMWVs of the scout platoons with M2A3s from the line companies to provide reconnaissance.

There were some issues identified, however. Most battalions identified the need for a stabilised machine gun for the Bradley commander, enhancing the ability to give suppressing fire all around the vehicle. Several also reported that they had damaged the main gun barrel in confined urban operations and requested a shorter 'urban operations barrel.' The experience of combat had also identified issues with the internal stowage, while the lack of a proper air conditioning unit meant that long periods of operating buttoned-up

(below) An M2A3 of 2-162 Infantry drives out of Patrol Base Volunteer in Sadr City during a QRF (Quick Response Force) mission. Note the prominent CIV, so vital to the Bradley's effectiveness in urban operations in Sadr City and elsewhere in Iraq. (US Army photo by SSgt. Ashley Brokop)

could degrade the effectiveness of the crew. Despite the praise heaped on the Bradley and its obvious effectiveness, there were still those who considered it obsolete for the wars that America would fight in the future. November 2003 saw the first deployment to Iraq of the Stryker Interim Combat vehicle, a multi-role eight-wheeled armoured vehicle, part of the new 'Objective Force' designed eventually to replace the 'Legacy Force' Abrams and Bradleys in the US Army. The deployment of the Stryker and the continued investment in the Future Combat System (FCS) programme took money away from the Bradley and the heavy armoured forces in general. In 2003-4, for example, the decision was taken not to the upgrade the M2A2 ODS and M3A2 ODS of 3rd Infantry Division and 3rd Armored Cavalry Regiment to A3 standard and use the money instead in the FCS programme. The developing tactical situation also put pressures on heavy forces in Iraq. The threat of IEDs and the need to up-armour the Army's fleet of wheeled armoured vehicles, principally the HMMWV, squeezed the resources available to support heavy armour. Indeed, the second rotation of US troops immediately following the invasion had to fight hard to bring all their heavy equipment in theatre. General Peter W. Chiarelli, commander of the 1st Cavalry Division, was at first prohibited from bringing all his Abrams and Bradleys to Iraq and had to enlist the personal support of General David D. Mckiernan, commander of land forces in Iraq, to get the decision reversed.

As the war changed into an increasingly desperate and sectarian insurgency the role of the Bradley too changed. Configured in its traditional role as part of the Armored Brigade, it continued to be valued for both its lethality and survivability. In June 2006, for example, 1st Brigade Combat Team, 1st Armored Division, arrived in Ramadi in Al Anbar province with 70 Abrams and 84 Bradleys. Instead of clearing the city block-by-block, as the US Army and Marines had done in Fallujah, the brigade established eighteen fire bases from which to mount aggressive patrols with their M1A1s and Bradleys. Joint patrols, employing Abrams, Bradleys, HMMWVs and dismounted infantry and tactics developed in the streets of Al Tharwa, Fallujah, Najaf and Sadr City, engaged insurgents at range of typically less than 200m and by early 2007 the insurgents' attacks on US forces had largely come to a stop.

From 2007, despite the introduction of improved belly armour, high power spotlights and other improvements as part of the Bradley Urban Survival Kit (BUSK), the Bradley was withdrawn from frontline combat in Iraq as the nature of the conflict changed. The prevalence of IEDs as the insurgents' main weapon against the US forces led to an investment in MRAPs (Mine Resistant Ambush Protected) of which the US procured some 12,000 between 2007 and 2012 for the wars in Iraq and Afghanistan. Nevertheless, the Bradley had again proved its worth. Some 150 Bradleys were destroyed by enemy action in Iraq, most of them lost to IEDs, but its firepower and protection proved an integral part in the success of US armoured forces, both militarily and psychologically, especially in the opening phases of the war.

((above) The familiar twin pillars of US armoured might in Iraq: an M1A1 Abrams and M3A2 ODS. Note the Bradley Reactive Armour Tiles, painted in CARC Tan, of this 1-4 Cavalry Bradley photographed during Operation Baton Rouge, an action designed to suppress the insurgency in the city of Samarra in October 2004. (US Army photo by SSgt. Shane A. Cuomo)

THE BRADLEY TODAY

The withdrawal from Iraq and the decision of the US Army to deploy only Stryker Brigade Combat Teams to Afghanistan might have been thought by some to have been the final chapter in the long decline of US armoured forces that had been apparent since the end of the Cold War. Despite the cancellation of the Future Combat Systems in 2009, the Bradley and the Abrams seemed to have had their day. In 2013 seven of the US Army's seventeen armoured brigades were de-activated. That policy changed in 2014 with the Russian annexation of Crimea and their interference in the subsequent civil war in Ukraine. Once again, the US and its NATO allies faced the prospect of a future conflict with a near-peer adversary. Operation Atlantic Resolve, the United States' show of commitment to their NATO allies saw American heavy armour return once more to Germany and a new emphasis on the Abrams and Bradley as the chief warfighting systems of the US Army's Maneuver Units in the shape of the Armored Brigade Combat Team (ABCT).

The US Army currently fields eleven ABCTs. This number was reached in 2019 by the conversion of 1st Brigade Combat Team, 1st Armored Division from Strykers to heavy armour. This is an increase in the 2016 projection made to Congress of a force of nine ABCTs by 2021. One of these ABCTs is stationed in South Korea, part of the US VIII Army, while another ABCT is stationed in Germany as part of the ongoing Operation Atlantic Resolve. To the end of 2020 there have been seven rotations as part of Operation Atlantic Resolve and 1st ABCT, 1st Cavalry Division is, at the time of writing, serving in this role. These regular units are supplemented by five ABCTs of the US Army National Guard which regularly serve alongside their regular counterparts on exercise in both the United States and in Europe.

The Armored Brigade Combat Team is a formidable fighting force of 4,700 soldiers. Its mission is simple: 'to disrupt or destroy enemy forces, control land areas … and be prepared to conduct combat operations to protect US national interests'. It currently fields four types of Bradley Fighting Vehicles: the M2A2 ODS or M2A3 IFV, the M3A3 CFV, the M7 BFIST and the Bradley ESV. Each ABCT contains two IFVs in its Brigade Headquarters, fourteen Bradley ESV in the Brigade Engineering Battalion, nine CFVs in the Brigade Reconnaissance Squadron, three CFV and two IFVs in the Headquarters Company of each armor and mechanized battalion, fourteen IFVs in each Rifle Company of the four mechanized infantry battalions, and four M7 BFISTs in the Fire Battalion. In 2015 there were 1,199 M2A3s and 453 M3A3s serving across the US Army's ABCTs, while 162 M2A3s, 62 M3A3s, 377 M2A2 ODS and 197 M3A2 ODS served in the National Guard units.

The Armored Brigade Combat Team is also a highly dynamic unit which responds quickly to changes identified in a rigorous and high-intensity training environment. For example, up until 2016 the ABCT's IFVs and tanks were organised into combined arms battalions. The change to armored and mechanized infantry battalions saw the reduction in strength of two rifle companies per brigade and an increase in the size of the brigade's reconnaissance squadron. This was mainly driven by a shortage in manpower, but it also led to changes in

(below) An M2A3 of 1-6 Infantry, 2nd ABCT, 1st Armored Division, patrols through northern Syria in support of Operation Inherent Resolve on 30 September 2020. (US Army photo by Sgt. 1st Class Curt Loter)

tactics across the brigade. The first unit to change its organisation was 3rd ABCT, 1st Cavalry Division and it tested the new formation at the National Training Center, Fort Irwin, CA, in the autumn of 2016.

Since 2015 US Army Bradleys have trained alongside Ukrainian armoured forces in Germany and alongside former Warsaw Pact adversaries and now NATO allies in Poland and Romania. They have trained in the former Soviet republic of Georgia as part of NATO's Georgian Defense Readiness Program. They continue to serve as a deterrent to aggression in the Korean Peninsula and have most recently begun to conduct high-profile patrols in north-west Syria as part of the continuing war against the Islamic State. In October 2020 3rd ABCT, 1st Cavalry Division became the first unit to accept delivery of the latest M2A4 IFV. The Bradley then remains, and is likely to remain for some time, at the heart of the Armored Brigade Combat Team and the US Army's warfighting capability.

(above) An M3A2 ODS of 6-8 Cavalry, the Brigade Reconnaissance Squadron of 2nd ABCT, 3rd Infantry Division, at the Hohenfels Training Area, Germany, during Exercise Combined Resolve XIV in September 2020. (US Army photo by Cpl. Shawn Pierce)

1-12 Cavalry, 3rd ABCT, 1st Cavalry Division, were the first unit to receive the new M2A4 IFV. This has the full BUSK III package and ECP II changes. (US Army photo by Sgt. Calab Franklin)

FURTHER READING

The best introduction to the development and early history of the Bradley is R.P. Hunnicutt's *Bradley: A History of American Fighting and Support Vehicles* (Novato, CA, 1999). In a similar vein, and somewhat more accessible, is Steve Zaloga's *M2/M3 Bradley Infantry Fighting Vehicle 1983-1995* (Osprey New Vanguard 18, 1995). A good photo album, covering the same period, is Jim Mesko, *M2/M3 Bradley in Action* (Squadron Signal: Carrollton, TX, 1992). A later, similar photo album which covers the period up to the war in Iraq is David Doyle, *M2/M3 Bradley* (Squadron Signal: Carrollton, TX, 2015). Michael Green and Greg Stewart's *M2/M3 Bradley* (Concord Firepower Pictorials 1010, 1990) is also a good reference for early Bradleys. Hans Halberstadt's *Bradley Company* (Crowood Press: Marlborough, 2001) is worth a look too. From a modeller's point of view, the best coverage of the Bradley up to the A2 is to be found in Verlinden's *Warmachines No. 5: 2/M3 Bradley*. Walter Böhm and Peter Siebert's *M2A2/M3A2 Bradley: Back of the US Mechanized Infantry* (Concord Mini Color Series 7506, 2002) has excellent coverage of the A2 and A2 ODS in the 1990s up to the eve of Iraq War. Ralph Zwilling's *M2A2 in Detail* (Wings and Wheels Publications, 2015) provides excellent reference on the M2A2 ODS. David Doyle's *Images of War: M2/M3 Bradley* (Pen & Sword Military, 2018) contains a very useful collection of walkarounds of the M2, M2A2 ODS and M3A2. For modellers wishing to detail the M3A2 or M3A3 then look no further than Sabot Publications' excellent two-volume *M2A3 Bradley Fighting Vehicle in Detail* (2018). This contains literally hundreds of photos of Bradleys both in Europe and

in the United States and has recently been republished by the Spanish company AMMO by Mig Jiménez.

German publisher Tankograd has produced a wide series of books on Cold War and contemporary US armour, many of which provide good references for Bradley enthusiasts. The most notable is Ralph Zwilling's *M2A3 Bradley* (Fast Track 3, 2014), but the following all have valuable material for modellers:

☐ Walter Böhm, R*EFORGER 1979-1985: Vehicles of the US Army during Exercises 'Return of Forces to Germany' Part 2* (American Special 3007, 2008)

☐ Walter Böhm, R*EFORGER 1986-1993: Vehicles of the US Army during Exercises 'Return of Forces to Germany' Part 3* (American Special 3008, 2008)

☐ Walter Böhm and Diego Ruiz Palmer, *REFORGER 87 Certain Strike: the Cold War's Largest Transatlantic Bridge* (American Special 3029, 2018)

☐ Walter Böhm, *Iron Brigade: 3rd Armored Brigade Combat Team, 4th (US) Infantry Division – German Tour 2017* (American Special 3034, 2019)

☐ Walter Böhm and Diego Ruiz Palmer, *REFORGER 85 Central Guardian: Winter War FTX against the Warsaw Pact* (American Special 3039, 2020)

☐ Björn Weber, *USAEUR: Vehicles and Units of the US Army in Europe 1992-2005* (American Special 3012, 2009)

☐ Ralph Zwilling, *Dagger Brigade: Army Rotational Force – Return of the 2nd Dagger Brigade* (American Special 3038, 2020)

My special gratitude to Mark Smith, Slawomir Zajackowski, MP Robinson, Torsten Wagner, Patrick Winnenpenninckx and Ralph Zwilling for contributing ideas, photographs and models to this volume. This volume would not have been possible without the resources of the Defense Visual Information Distribution Service (DVIDS) and the US National Archives

The armoured fist of the US Army in Europe: an M1A2 SEP V2 and M2A3 of 3-66 Armor, 1st ABCT, 1st Infantry Division, prepare to take part in a live-fire exercise at the Grafenwoehr Training Area during Exercise Combined Resolve XII in August 2019. (US Army photo by Sgt. Randis Monroe)